PONS

Die drei ???®

Soccer Gangsters

von Brigitte Johanna Henkel-Waidhofer

PONS GmbH
Stuttgart

PONS

Die drei ???®

Soccer Gangsters

von Brigitte Johanna Henkel-Waidhofer
Englisch von Patricia Wolf

basierend auf „Die drei ??? - Fußball Gangster" von
Brigitte Johanna Henkel-Waidhofer

Based on characters by Robert Arthur.

Auflage A1 5 4 3 2 1 / 2012 2011 2010 2009

Produktinfos und Online-Shop: www.pons.de
E-Mail: info@pons.de
Online-Wörterbuch und Online-Bildwörterbuch: www.pons.eu

Annotationen und Übungen: Patricia Wolf
Redaktion: Elizabeth Webster, Karin Adam
Logoentwurf: Erwin Poell, Heidelberg
Logoüberarbeitung: Sabine Redlin, Ludwigsburg
Titelillustration: Silvia Christoph, Berlin
Einbandgestaltung: Daniel Müller, Stuttgart
Tonaufnahmen/Digital Mastering: allegria Musik-/Audioproduktion GbR
Sprecherin: Elizabeth Webster
Layout/Satz: Satz und mehr, Besigheim
Druck und Bindung: L.E.G.O. S.p.A., Lavis (TN)

Printed in Italy.
ISBN: 978-3-12-010045-4

Inhaltsverzeichnis

Inhaltsangabe

Welches Interesse könnte ein Lebensmittelkonzern daran haben, eine ganze Fußballmannschaft unter seine Kontrolle zu bringen? Jimboy, Justus' Cousin, hat sich mächtig verändert, seit er Stürmer in dieser Elf ist. Und zwar nicht zu seinem Vorteil. Die drei ??? bemerken bald einen Zusammenhang zwischen Jimboys Schweigsamkeit und seinen Erlebnissen im streng bewachten Trainingslager. Aber kaum haben sie Erfolg bei ihren Erkundungen, schaltet sich Inspektor Cotta ein. Justus, Peter und Bob sollen die Finger von dem brandheißen Fall lassen. Das sehen die drei ??? entschieden anders...

Auftretende Personen

Justus Jonas – „The First Investigator“
ist der Anführer der drei ??? und weiß nicht nur alles über die Nibelungen.

Peter Shaw – „The Second Investigator“
ist der Zweite Detektiv, supersportlich und auch sonst immer gut drauf.

Bob Andrews – „ The Third Investigator“
spielt keinesfalls die dritte Geige; sondern ist unter anderem immer vorneweg, wenn's um Technik geht, und hat einen ganz großen Auftritt als Verkleideter.

Lys, Elizabeth und Kelly
sind – in dieser Reihenfolge – die Freundinnen der drei Jungen.

Titus Jonas
ist Justus' Onkel und betreibt den Schrottplatz, auf dem das Hauptquartier der drei ??? steht.

Tante Mathilda
ist seine Frau und schon wegen ihres Kirschkuchens äußerst populär.

Jimboy
ist ein Vetter von Justus, ein Fußballstar von morgen und benimmt sich schon mal sehr seltsam.

Eric Randolphe
ist ein Fernsehjournalist, dem das Übertragen von Sportereignissen nicht genügt.

Harry Bow
ist mal ziemlich redselig und dann wieder überhaupt nicht.

Mike Hammer
weiß als Sportpädagoge alles über Fußball und kennt noch ein paar Tricks mehr.

Tamara Mostowsky
ist in ihrem Beruf absolut professionell und scheint ziemlich nett zu sein.

Inspektor Cotta
ist von der Polizei in Rocky Beach und der Ansicht, die drei ??? müssten sich aus diesem Fall raushalten – aber da ist es schon zu spät.

1. An Evil[1] Foul

Peter was in extreme pain. Justus saw the Second Investigator fall down in slow-motion[2].
"Peter!" Justus screamed, but his friend couldn't hear him. Taking big strides[3] he ran down the narrow[4] stone steps and almost bumped into[5] Elizabeth and Kelly. The girls belonged to the medical team that takes care of injured[6] players. They were running onto the playing field behind two men carrying a stretcher[7]. Justus wanted to follow them, but a boy with an armband[8] held him back. "Not you," he said rudely[9] "you don't belong here[10]." Justus gave him a dirty look[11] but stopped at the side line. He could see Peter's belly quickly moving up and down. Kelly was worried[12] and bent over her friend.
Almost all of the players jogged up to them and stood in a circle around the injured boy. The referee[13] signaled to the helpers to hurry. Justus felt his anger growing. Here was a seriously injured player lying on the ground and this jerk[14], was reacting as cool as a cucumber[15].

1 evil: böse, hinterhältig
2 slow-motion: Zeitlupe
3 stride: großer Schritt
4 narrow: eng
5 to bump into: anrempeln
6 injured: verletzt
7 stretcher: Tragbahre
8 armband: Armbinde
9 rudely: unhöflich
10 you don't belong here: du gehörst nicht hierher, hast hier nichts zu suchen
11 dirty look: böser Blick
12 worried: besorgt
13 referee: Schiedsrichter
14 jerk: Schnösel, Trottel
15 cool as a cucumber: kalt wie ein Fisch *(Redewendung)*

"Idiot," he hissed[1]. Carefully they lifted Peter onto the stretcher. Then the helpers and their patient disappeared[2] behind the wide swinging doors into the first aid room[3].

Justus wasn't interested in soccer[4] until his high school team made the varsity league[5]. The rules weren't hard to understand for him, but he still wasn't a real fan. He was only half interested in today's match as well. The only reason he came along was because Peter had become the midfield-star[6] of the team in the past weeks.

"Hey!" Justus went back to the boy from the security squad[7]. "How did that happen?"

The other boy looked at him with pity[8]. "During the counterattack[9] after the corner ball, the boy from the 'Angels' covering[10]on the left missed a cross[11]." He seemed to use as many special technical terms[12] as possible. He wanted to show off[13] as an expert of the new favorite sport of many teenagers and also wanted to make Justus angry. "Your man got the ball and the Angels' sweeper[14] swept him away."

"Well, they're stupid to still play with a sweeper, it's really old-fashioned[15]!" the First Investigator said. He wanted to stand up to this show-off. At the same moment the door of the first aid room opened and Kelly stormed out. "It's probably the cruciate ligament[16]," she

1 to hiss: zischen, fauchen
2 to disappear: verschwinden
3 first aid room: Erste Hilfe Raum
4 soccer (US): Fußball
5 varsity league: oberste Liga der Schule, Liga der Universität, Hochschule
6 had become the mid-field star: war der Mittelfeld-Star geworden
7 security squad: Sicherheitsdienst
8 pity: Mitleid
9 counterattack: Gegenangriff, Konter
10 covering: decken
11 cross: Flanke
12 technical term: Fachausdruck
13 to show off: angeben
14 sweeper: Libero
15 old-fashioned: altmodisch
16 cruciate ligament: Kreuzband

called, "it's either[1] overstretched or a bit torn[2]. He has to be x-rayed[3]."

"I have a problem," Justus said. "I would like to go along to the hospital but my cousin is arriving today. He is staying with us for a while. I promised Uncle Titus to go along to the airport."

"No problem," Kelly said. "Elizabeth and I will go along with Peter. We'll call you afterwards, okay?"

Justus nodded[4] and was relieved[5]. In the past he often felt that both girls and their whole cheerleading squad[6] were quite complicated. But that changed[7] totally ever since Bob and Peter's girl-friends started playing soccer. They were also responsible[8] for organizing tournaments.[9]

02 Two hours later Justus and Uncle Titus were standing in the airport waiting area. Because the air traffic controllers[10] at the airport were on strike, the chaos here was worse than usual. Several signs were up about the strike – the air traffic controllers wanted to have more breaks during working time and they needed more workers. A few weeks ago there was almost a collision in the sky over Los Angeles. The result of the investigation[11] showed that it was the fault[12] of an overtired air traffic controller in the tower[13].

1 either ... or: entweder ... oder
2 torn: gerissen
3 to x-ray: röntgen
4 to nod: nicken
5 relieved: erleichtert
6 cheerleading squad: Cheerleader Gruppe, die während des Spiels tanzt und die Mannschaft anfeuert
7 changed: änderte sich
8 responsible: verantwortlich
9 tournament: Turnier
10 air traffic controller: Fluglotse
11 investigation: Untersuchung
12 fault: Schuld
13 tower: Kontrollturm

"Have I ever met Jimboy before[1]?" asked Justus.
Uncle Titus shook his head. "Aunt Mathilda and I were in Chicago after he was born. But you weren't around yet. [2]"
Aunt Mathilda already told Justus about the complicated relationships[3] between his relatives[4]. His mother and Jimboy's father had a mutual[5] father, who was Uncle Titus' father's brother. Understanding this was no problem for Justus, the mastermind[6]. Justus wanted to explain to Peter and Bob how he was related to[7] Jimboy. But they waved it off and said they didn't care.
"I can't wait to see if we look alike," the First Investigator said.
"I doubt[8] it," Uncle Titus said. "Jimboy's father, Derny, is very, very tall. He's two feet taller than anyone else in the family. Jimboy inherited[9] his talent for soccer from him."
When the first travellers came out of the gate Justus craned[10] his neck to get a better view. The first one he saw was a blond guy, who seemed really nice. He had a duffle bag[11] and was wearing cowboy boots. But he didn't even look at Uncle Titus. Justus knew that Jimboy had Uncle Titus' photograph with him so he wouldn't miss him. Next, a red-haired boy in a track-suit[12] came along, who was looking at the people waiting.
"Hi," a deep voice on their right suddenly said, "I'm James Jonas."

1 have I ever met him before: habe ich ihn jemals zuvor getroffen
2 weren't around yet : noch nicht da
3 relationship: Beziehung
4 relative: Verwandter
5 mutual: gemeinsam
6 mastermind: Computerhirn, Genie
7 related to: verwandt mit
8 to doubt something: anzweifeln
9 to inherit: erben
10 to crane: recken, strecken
11 duffle bag: Kleidersack, Seemannsbeutel
12 track-suit: Trainingsanzug

Justus looked around surprised. He had seen the tall guy with the long ponytail[1] when he came out, but never thought he could be his athletic cousin. He looked more like a musician or a painter.
"I'm Titus Jonas," Uncle Titus said, "and this is your cousin Justus."
"Hello, Jimboy." Justus and Jonas shook hands and smiled.
"Jimboy?" he repeated. "Nobody in Chicago calls me 'Jimboy' anymore."
"Here we always call you that when we talk about you. Do you mind[2]?" Justus asked. They were walking to the baggage claim area[3]. James shook his head[4]. "Actually[5] no," he answered. "Maybe it's not too bad to say goodbye to 'James'."
Even though Jimboy was only five months older than Justus, he was much taller. He was wearing baggy[6] jeans and a casual sweater[7]. But you could tell he was in good shape[8]. They fetched Jimboy's duffle bag and fought[9] their way through the crowd to the exit[10]. A few minutes later they turned onto the highway[11].
"Have you ever been on the West coast before?" Justus asked. Jimboy said no.
"Have you ever been in the East?" Jimboy asked. This time Justus shook his head.
Jimboy wanted to stay in Rocky Beach to attend Tamilton High School[12] for at least half a year. The school's varsity soccer team was famous all the way down to Mexico.

1 ponytail: Pferdeschwanz
2 to mind: etwas ausmachen
3 baggage claim area: Gepäckausgabe
4 to shake one's head: den Kopf schütteln
5 actually: eigentlich, tatsächlich
6 baggy: locker, weit
7 casual sweater: lässiger/sportlicher Pullover
8 in good shape: fit, trainiert
9 fought: kämpften
10 exit: Ausgang
11 highway: Autobahn
12 to attend High School: das Gymnasium besuchen

Next weekend a national tournament with the best soccer talents would take place to promote[1] the new professional league. And Jimboy was so talented he was chosen[2] out of hundreds of candidates in Chicago.

"I want to become a professional soccer player," he said. "And I'm quite sure I can make it[3]."

Justus liked his self-confident attitude[4]. "We'll get along[5] great," he thought.

Of course Jimboy knew that Justus had a successful[6] detective agency with two friends. But that was all he knew, so Justus told him all about the Three Investigators.

"We can't count on[7] Peter at the moment," he finally said. "He was the victim[8] of an evil foul this afternoon."

"You guys play soccer too?" Jimboy said happily. Justus nodded. "Peter is quite good. But he surely can't compare with[9] you."

"On the other hand I can't solve crime cases[10]," Jimboy said. Justus continued his report about Justus, Peter and Bob and their headquarters[11] in an old converted trailer.[12] It stood in a lonely corner of Uncle Titus' junkyard[13] in Rocky Beach. He told him about their technical equipment[14] which included an answering machine, a fax machine and a light-weight laptop with an integrated webcam. When they

1 to promote: für etwas werben
2 was chosen: wurde gewählt
3 to make it: es schaffen
4 selfconfident attitude: selbstbewusste Einstellung
5 to get along: miteinander auskommen
6 successful: erfolgreich
7 to count on someone: auf jmd. zählen
8 victim: Opfer
9 to compare with: sich vergleichen
10 solve crime cases: Kriminalfälle lösen
11 headquarters: Hauptquartier
12 converted trailer: umgebauter Wohnwagen
13 junkyard: Schrottplatz
14 equipment: Ausrüstung

arrived, first of all Jimboy wanted a tour. He was impressed[1] by the equipment. But when Justus opened the door to the secret passage[2] his cousin was speechless[3].

"That is our tunnel number two," the First Investigator explained in a matter-of-fact way[4]. "It leads halfway underneath the junkyard in case we have to leave the headquarters quickly."

"Is what you do dangerous?"

Justus winked[5] at him. "We used it to escape[6] Aunt Mathilda more than anything else."

"I understand," Jimboy laughed.

"We have another secret passage. That one takes us away from the junkyard without being seen." Justus closed the trap door[7]. "Follow me!"

They went through the back entrance and walked around the outside of the wooden fence, which had a big painting on it. He put his finger in the dog's eye in the painting, which was actually a knothole[8]. A narrow door opened.

"Great!" Jimboy was again impressed. "I'd also like to meet your friends soon."

Before they fell asleep, Justus talked about Peter, Bob, their friends Lys, Kelly and Elizabeth for a long time. He also told him about Inspector Cotta – a man they often co-operated with. And about Morton, the chauffeur of a Rolls Royce. The Three Investigators could use his service whenever they needed it – thanks to a multi-millionaire client they once had[9].

1 impressed: beindrückt
2 secret passage: Geheimgang
3 speechless: sprachlos
4 matter-of-fact way: sachliche Art und Weise
5 to wink: zwinkern
6 to escape: flüchten
7 trap door: Falltür
8 knothole: Astloch
9 they once had: den sie früher hatten

Jimboy also wanted to know what their most exciting case so far[1] had been. Justus waved his hand. “We’ve often asked ourselves that question,” said Justus, “and we always come to the same conclusion[2]: it’s the case we’re solving[3] at the moment. And we expect[4] the next one to be even more exciting.”
“It’s just like soccer,” Jimboy yawned[5], “the next game is always the hardest.”

Detective question 1

Welcome Ausrüstung würdest du anschaffen, um ein perfektes Detektivbüro mit allem drum und dran einzurichten?

1 so far: bis jetzt
2 conclusion: Schlussfolgerung
3 to solve: lösen
4 to expect: erwarten
5 to yawn: gähnen

2. Explosive News

They decided to play on a small field with two center forwards[1] and three defenders[2]. Bob and Jimboy tried to score goals[3] while the girls took over the defense. Justus pulled two benches[4] onto the field for goals. Peter was the referee. For the kick-off[5] he pretended[6] to blow an imaginary whistle[7] in a dramatic way. Soon it was clear that Jimboy really was an ace[8] at soccer. He always stayed close on the ball, dribbled past his opponents[9] any way he chose to[10], cleverly bluffed and kicked the ball into the improvised soccer goal four times.
Some students from the Three Investigators' high school[11] watched the scene and wanted to know who this guy was and where he came from. Justus proudly[12] introduced his cousin.
"He will probably have a great career," Justus heard one school mate say. "Only too bad," said another boy, "he specialised in soccer of all things. There's no money in that profession[13]."
After they took a shower[14] all seven of them went to a small café across the street. They ordered soft-drinks[15] and burgers[16]. "Do you

1 center forward: Mittelstürmer
2 defender: Verteidiger
3 to score a goal: ein Tor schießen
4 bench: Bank
5 kick-off: Anstoß
6 to pretend: so tun als ob
7 whistle: Trillerpfeife
8 ace: Ass
9 opponent: Gegner
10 anyway he chose to: so wie er wollte
11 high school: entspricht dem Gymnasium
12 proud: stolz
13 profession: Beruf
14 shower: Dusche
15 soft-drink: Erfrischungsgetränk
16 burger: Hamburger *(Abkürzung)*

really think that you can earn enough money by playing soccer?" Justus asked.

Jimboy nodded. "But a lot depends on[1] the next soccer world championship. If enough people become enthusiastic about soccer then there'll soon be a better professional soccer league in the USA." He looked around. "And then I'll be one of them."

"I don't think so," Bob disagreed[2]. "The first attempt[3] to make soccer popular here was a big flop. Even though world-famous players like Pelé played in New York."

Kelly didn't agree. She said that, in the past[4], they forgot about the schools. And that nobody took care of youth work[5] and the young and upcoming[6] talents in our own country.

"You seem to know a lot about it." Jimboy was very impressed. Kelly smiled shyly and twirled her ponytail.

Justus was thinking about Jimboy's performance and the conversation that they had afterwards when he was looking at his cousin's documents in the office an hour later. "Like a male model[7]," he said to himself. It was a proper application folder[8], with glossy photographs, CV[9], winner-certificates[10] from tournaments that he participated[11] in, a detailed list of all results of sports-medical examinations. Jimboy successfully applied[12] at Tamilton High School with this portfolio. The school was connected to a college[13] where he could con-

1 to depend on: davon abhängen
2 to disagree: nicht übereinstimmen
3 attempt: Versuch
4 in the past: damals
5 youth work: Sozialarbeit mit Jugendlichen
6 upcoming: aufstrebend
7 male model: männliches Fotomodell
8 application folder: Bewerbungsmappe
9 CV: curriculum vitae, Lebenslauf
10 certificate: Urkunde
11 to participate: teilnehmen
12 to apply: sich bewerben
13 college: Hochschule

tinue, if he received good grades[1] at school – without missing out[2] on soccer.
Aunt Mathilda came and brought one of her famous cherry pies. Justus looked down at himself and was satisfied that he could afford[3] this luxury without a bad conscience[4] – after all, he had slimmed down[5] lately because of his girlfriend, Lys, and all the exercise[6] he'd been getting. Then he saw the two letters that the mailman put under the door. Justus took the letter opener and opened one of the envelopes. Inside was an advertisement[7] for stationery paper[8].
"Where did they possibly get our address?" he murmured[9]. At the same time he took the other envelope. He opened the envelope with the letter opener and there was suddenly a deafening[10] bang.
He was pushed back into the chair as if a big force[11] held him there. At the same time a terrible smell[12] overwhelmed[13] him. His eyes started to water. Justus struggled out of the chair and stumbled[14] to the door.
Outside he took a few deep breaths. Then he looked around. Nobody noticed[15] him. Nobody heard the sound of the explosion. The trucks nearby were making a lot of noise because they were unloading big rocks. They were working for hours.

1 grade (US): Schulnote
2 to miss out on something: etwas verpassen
3 to afford: sich leisten
4 conscience: Gewissen
5 to slim down: abnehmen
6 exercise: Bewegung
7 advertisement: Anzeige
8 stationery paper: Briefpapier
9 to murmur: murmeln
10 deafening: ohrenbetäubend
11 force: Kraft
12 smell: Geruch
13 to overwhelm: überfluten, überwältigen
14 to stumble: stolpern
15 to notice: bemerken

He turned back around towards the trailer. Slowly gray smoke was drifting[1] away through the open door. Justus was surprised that nothing was destroyed[2]. He pinched his nose shut[3], returned to the office, took the letter opener and picked up the shredded envelope with it. Then he went outside again and pulled a rag[4] out of his pocket. He held the envelope between his thumb and forefinger with the rag and took out the almost undamaged[5] white piece of paper from inside.

"FRYDAY FUUTBALL FINDS FALSE FRIENDS[6]" was written there. Justus saw right away that each of the letters was cut out of newspapers and that someone meant soccer, not football. "FAFNIR FIRES FIRESTONE ON FANS!"

05 Twenty minutes later Bob's orange VW-beetle drove into the junkyard. Justus immediately alarmed[7] the specialist for research[8], investigation technology and documentation.

"What a mess[9]!" Bob said, wrinkled his nose[10] and took a look at the hate mail[11]. The postmark[12] showed that the letter was posted in Los Angeles two days before. He carefully sprinkled gray powder on the piece of paper. "Maybe we're lucky[13] and there will be nice and clear fingerprints[14]," he said to himself. He repeated the same procedure with the envelope. Then he took out a small piece of cardboard[15] with

1 to drift: treiben
2 destroyed: zerstört
3 to pinch one's nose shut: sich die Nase zuhalten
4 rag: Lappen
5 undamaged: unbeschädigt
6 *korrekte Schreibweise*: Friday, football
7 to alarm someone: jmd. alarmieren
8 research: Forschung
9 mess: *hier*: Schweinerei
10 to wrinkle one's nose: die Nase rümpfen
11 hate mail: Drohbrief
12 postmark: Poststempel
13 to be lucky: Glück haben
14 fingerprints: Fingerabdrücke
15 cardboard: Karton

a pair of pincers[1]. He nodded and showed Justus the fuse[2] that was attached[3] to the cardboard. Then he put the envelope into a transparent folder[4], sat down at the desk and took a closer look at the fuse mechanism with a magnifying glass[5].
"What do you think?" Justus bent over him from behind.
"The smelly powder was inside a plastic tube[6]. And the tube was connected[7] to the envelope by a thread[8]. When you cut it with the letter opener the whole thing went off."
"So some kind of explosive[9] was mixed with the smelly powder," Justus concluded[10].
"And it was exactly the right dose." Bob put the magnifying glass aside. "Somebody was at work here who knew exactly what he was doing. I'll take a closer look at the powder." He stood up and disappeared behind the thick laboratory curtain[11].
Justus called after him. First of all they had to find out which newspapers the letters were from. "It would be great if we could find out the date of the newspapers."
Bob came back. "That'll take a while, by then I'll know the mixture ratio[12] of the ingredients[13]." He bent over Justus' shoulder. "The sender is definitely[14] not a soccer fan. But he likes alliterations[15]." Sur-

1 pair of pincers: Pinzette
2 fuse: Zünder
3 attached: befestigt
4 transparent folder: Klarsichthülle
5 magnifying glass: Lupe
6 tube: Röhrchen
7 connected: verbunden
8 thread: Faden
9 explosive: Sprengstoff
10 to conclude: schlussfolgern
11 laboratory curtain: Vorhang im Labor
12 mixture ratio: Mischungsverhältnis
13 ingredient: Zutat
14 definitely: ganz bestimmt
15 alliteration: Alliteration – eine Folge von Wörtern mit dem gleichen Anfangsbuchstaben

prised Justus looked at his friend. ‘Alliterations?’ Since when does Bob Andrews know such fancy words?

Annoyed,[1] Bob frowned[2]. Of course Justus Jonas was an absolute ace at almost every topic[3]. But did he have to react so arrogantly when someone else knew something? Bob liked the word ‘alliteration’ when he heard it in class for the first time. He memorized[4]: ‘alliterations’ were a number of words in a phrase starting with the same letter. And he also remembered that alliterations were popular among poets[5] and in advertising. Bob swallowed[6] his anger because there was one part of the hate mail he really couldn’t figure out[7]. “But you surely know who or what this Fafnir is.”

Justus had probably just been waiting for that question. Without stopping for breath he talked about the myth of the Nibelungs[8]– the treasure[9] that the dragon[10] Fafnir protected[11] until Siegfried killed it. And thanks to the dragon blood he could only be wounded in one single spot.

Bob pointed to[12] the letter. “I see. And our pen pal[13] also knows all of that?”

“Why does it have to be a ‘he’?”

Bob wiped a strand of hair[14] off his forehead. “Girls don’t usually say no to soccer.”

1 annoyed: genervt, verärgert
2 to frown: Stirnrunzeln, Mundwinkel herunterziehen
3 topic: Thema
4 to memorize: auswendig lernen
5 poet: Dichter
6 to swallow: schlucken
7 to figure out: verstehen, enträtseln
8 myth of the Nibelungs: Nibelungensage
9 treasure: Schatz
10 dragon: Drache
11 to protect: beschützen
12 to point to: auf etw. zeigen
13 pen pal: Brieffreund
14 strand of hair: Haarsträhne

Justus pinched his lower lip, as always when he was thinking hard. "You're right. Take our school. More and more people are interested in soccer. First the girls were keen on it[1] and then the guys."
"Maybe they are enthusiastic about it because their parents don't have a say in it," Bob said. "In the States[2] almost everybody plays baseball, football and basketball. Soccer is something quite[3] new. Kelly's, Lys' and Elizabeth's enthusiasm was contagious[4] as well."
The First Investigator nodded. "I read in the school's newsletter that recently a lot of high schools and colleges reduced the budget of other sports in favor of[5] soccer."
"Well, okay," said Bob, "but what have we got to do with that? Why do they send us stink bombs?"
Jimboy spread out a blanket[6] and they sat down on it.
"In there," he said and pointed over his shoulder to the trailer, "it still smells awful[7]." He looked at Justus attentively[8]. "Is there a lot of rivalry[9] between the soccer, football and baseball fans in Rocky Beach?" "If anything, then between the clubs. But for the fans of different kinds of sports to fight with each other – that's a first[10]."
"Not in Chicago. There is an old feud[11] between baseball and basketball players."
06 Peter and Bob elegantly rode into the junkyard on their bikes. Justus got to the point[12] right away. "Do you know anything about rivalry between the fans of different kinds of sports here?" The Second

1 to be keen on something: scharf auf etwas sein
2 States: Abkürzung für United States of America
3 quite: ziemlich
4 contagious: ansteckend
5 in favor of: zugunsten von
6 blanket: Decke
7 awful: schrecklich, entsetzlich
8 attentive: aufmerksam
9 rivalry: Rivalität
10 a first: das erste Mal
11 feud: Fehde, Kleinkrieg
12 to get to the point: auf den Punkt kommen, ohne Umschweife

Investigator shook his head. Bob shrugged[1] and took the thick stack[2] of newspapers off the back of his bike without answering. "My dad sends his regards[3]. He wishes us luck."
Mr Andrews was a journalist at the Los Angeles Post and had brought his son all the newspapers from Rocky Beach and the surrounding[4] areas of the past days.
"I found out about the glue[5]," said Bob. "Just as we expected, an absolutely ordinary brand[6]. We can't trace that back[7] to the sender."
All four of them eagerly[8] worked on the countless headlines[9]. And they were soon successful. Too successful. They actually found six of the ten different 'Fs' in five different newspapers. "That doesn't lead[10] us anywhere," Justus was annoyed. "You'll just have to come along on Friday," said Jimboy.
"Why?"asked Bob. "Come along where?"
"It says here "FRYDAY FUUTBALL[11] FINDS FALSE FRIENDS" Jimboy read slowly. "The big tournament in the Rose Bowl[12] in Pasadena is on Friday. That's the reason[13] that I'm here at all."
When they drew straws[14] about who should go in which car, Justus won twice. Not only did he draw Peter's convertible[15], but Lys was

1 to shrug: Achselzucken
2 stack: Stapel
3 to send someone's regards: Grüße ausrichten
4 surrounding: umliegend
5 glue: Klebstoff
6 ordinary brand: gewöhnliche Marke
7 to trace something back: zurückverfolgen
8 eager: eifrig
9 headline: Überschrift
10 to lead: führen
11 football: *(British English)* Fußball, *(US)*American Football
12 Rose Bowl: *(hier)* Name eines Stadions
13 reason: Grund
14 to draw straws: Streichhölzchen ziehen, auslosen
15 convertible: Kabrio(lett), Auto mit Faltdach

also joining[1] him. Lys de Kerk was a successful teenage actress[2] in Hollywood before she interrupted[3] her career to go to college. Justus was very impressed by the blond girl. She always managed[4] to surprise him with her knowledge. She also knew immediately who Fafnir was.

07 The Rose Bowl had room for almost 100,000 people. Not quite that many people came to the junior tournament of 'Victoria', the sporting goods manufacturer[5]. The seats in a lot of rows were occupied. The company convinced many schools in and around Los Angeles to give the kids a day off[6].

The semi-finals[7] were the next thing on the program, after the preliminary rounds[8] in the morning.

"Watch Jimboy!" Lys told Justus." The way he plays is really something to look at."

"Yes!" screamed Peter. "Goal! Your cousin is simply awesome[9]!" He thumped[10] Justus' shoulder. "If he continues to play like that he'll be able to compete[11] on Sunday."

"I'm sure he'll play on Sunday,"Kelly said. "Wanna[12] bet[13] on it?" She offered Justus her hand but he acted as if[14] he didn't see her.

1 to join someone: mitgehen
2 actress: Schauspielerin
3 to interrupt: unterbrechen
4 to manage something: etw. schaffen
5 manufacturer: Hersteller
6 a day off: ein freier Tag
7 semi-finals: Halbfinale
8 preliminary round: Vorrunde
9 awesome: super, fantastisch
10 thump: freundschaftlich daraufschlagen
11 to compete: am Wettbewerb teilnehmen
12 wanna: *'want to'(Umgangssprache)*: möchtest du
13 to bet: wetten
14 to act as if: tun als ob

Down on the lawn the team mates celebrated[1] Jimboy. After the whistle[2] Justus concentrated totally on his cousin for a few minutes. He moved even more smoothly than during the game a couple of days ago. But Justus also noticed two of his team mates: an extremely quick defender who dangerously appeared[3] in attacks again and again – plus the goalkeeper[4]. He thought about the hate mail. "This goalkeeper on Jimboy's team could just as well[5] play in an American football team, don't you think?" he asked.
"Sure," Peter answered. Then he looked at Justus. "Do you think the football players are afraid of losing[6] players to the professional soccer league, once it starts?"
"Could be possible, couldn't it?"

Jimboy arrived at the parking lot half an hour late for the ride home. "Sorry," he said, but he didn't look guilty[7] at all. "Can you imagine[8], they hired[9] me straight from the dressing-room! On Monday I'm going to a training camp at Silverwood Lake."
"Who hired you?" Justus asked.
"Well, who do you think?" Aunt Mathilda interrupted, "Some athletic club of course."
Then Uncle Titus informed her that the athletic clubs didn't call the shots[10] in sports anymore. Large companies bought teams for a lot of money. And then Uncle Titus talked about 'the good old times' when he also played soccer. "In former times[11] we played ball every-

1 to celebrate: feiern
2 whistle: Anpfiff
3 to appear: auftauchen
4 goalkeeper: Torwart
5 just as well: *hier:* genausogut
6 to lose: verlieren
7 guilty: schuldig
8 to imagine: sich vorstellen
9 to hire: einstellen
10 to call the shots: das Sagen haben *(umgangssprachlich)*
11 former times: frühere Zeiten

where," he remembered. "On the street, in the school yard and in front of the garage. And then American football and baseball became popular. After that soccer seemed boring and much too European. And finally the advertising[1] on TV started. Then it was all over. Because, as you know, a soccer match can't be interrupted for commercial breaks[2] every 10-15 minutes."

After consulting[3] Aunt Mathilda's friend who was a lawyer[4], Jimboy signed the contract[5]. The food corporation 'Smell', with branches[6] all over the world, was obligated[7] to teach, accommodate[8] and supply medical care for Jimboy – at their own boarding school for athletes for two years. On top of that, the company would pay $10,000 per year – plus the bonus for winning a game. In return[9] Jimboy should play 40 games per season[10] and take part in promotional events. Jimboy was surprised by the conversation. He told them that his good grades at school hardly made an impression[11] on the managers from the Californian 'Smell' plant[12] in Fresno.
"That should happen to me some day," Bob said enviously[13] on the way to the finals in Pasadena. His grades dropped during the last school term[14]. But this term his report card[15] was quite decent[16]. His

1 advertising: Werbung
2 commercial break: Werbepause
3 to consult: beraten lassen
4 lawyer: Rechtsanwalt/in
5 to sign a contract: einen Vertrag unterschreiben
6 branch: Filiale, Zweigstelle
7 obligated: verpflichtet
8 accommodate: Unterkunft geben
9 in return: im Gegenzug
10 season: *hier* Saison
11 impression: Eindruck
12 plant: Fabrik
13 envious: neidisch
14 school term: Schulhalbjahr
15 report card: Schulzeugnis
16 decent: anständig

parents were very strict and put the pressure on[1]. He should either improve his grades or quit[2] his part-time job at the music agency "Sax Sendler". But that really wasn't an option for him, because he wanted to become a music manager.
There was even more activity around the stadium than on Friday. It took Peter a quarter of an hour to find a parking space. When Justus saw the girls at the meeting-point he knew at once[3] that something was wrong.
"I received hate mail," said Kelly and offered Justus a briefcase[4]. The First Investigator opened the latch[5] and the content of the briefcase slid out. All six of them stared at the piece of paper. Again letters were cut out of newspapers. "BASEBALL BEGS[6] BAGGIO'S BITTER BANANAS," the message announced[7] this time.

Jimboy's team won the tournament, but only with lots of luck after a penalty shoot-out[8]. They were all very happy when he came back to Rocky Beach in the evening.
In the meantime the Three Investigators were busy investigating Kelly's hate mail. This letter didn't have any fingerprints[9] on it, unlike[10] the first one. But the mechanism catapulting the smelly powder was identical. And the powder mixture was identical as well. "We all have to watch out when we open our letters in the next few days," Justus said. "I have a feeling that we might get more of these."
"If there are more explosives inside, it could be quite dangerous."

1 to put pressure on: Druck ausüben
2 to quit: aufhören, aufgeben
3 at once: sofort
4 briefcase: Aktentasche
5 latch: Verschluss
6 to beg: betteln
7 to announce: ankündigen
8 penalty shoot-out: Elfmeterschießen
9 fingerprint:Fingerabdruck
10 unlike: im Gegensatz zu

Kelly read the message[1] to them.
"What a bunch of baloney,[2]" Jimboy commented with his mouth full. "He would never change over to baseball."
"Who?" Surprised, Justus looked at his cousin.
"Why Baggio, of course. Roberto Baggio."
"None of us know him," Bob interrupted.
Lys threw back her long blond hair. "I do. An Italian forward who converted to Buddhism[3]."
"Correct" Jimboy nodded towards Lys. "Italy's most expensive forward. He plays at AC Milan, is a Buddhist and has a ..." He stopped talking and looked around confused.
"And has what?"
"... a pony-tail." Jimboy pointed to his hair. "Like me!"
Justus looked at his cousin. "Then the letters could have something to do with you," he said slowly.
Without waiting for a reaction he told them about alliterations and the conclusions they came to now. "That's all fine!" Jimboy interrupted, "But what's the point? It's all about different ball games and obviously[4] somebody can't stand[5] soccer."
"Maybe it is about you," Peter corrected. "You played on Friday and you also have a pony-tail."
"We'll just have to be patient[6]," Justus said. "The sender has a plan. He hasn't reached his goal yet. That's why he'll continue." He grinned[7]. "Maybe next with: Soccer spoils star's style[8]."
"Or: Justus Jonas jogs joylessly[9]," Kelly answered.

1 message: Nachricht
2 baloney: Unsinn *(Redewendung)*
3 to convert to Buddhism: zum Buddhismus übertreten
4 obviously: offensichtlich
5 can't stand: nicht ausstehen können
6 patient: geduldig
7 to grin: grinsen
8 soccer spoils star's style: Fußball verdirbt den guten Stil des Stars
9 joyless: freudlos

"Kelly cracks[1] crime cases," the First Investigator shot back.
"Investigator inquires[2]…" Kelly continued.
"That's enough!" Peter shouted.
"Peter protests pedantically," Elizabeth giggled[3].

Because the girls had volunteered[4] to help make the preparations for the graduation[5] party, the Three Investigators drove to the boarding school[6] with Jimboy. "Most tourists only know the city, Hollywood and the film studios or Disneyland," Peter explained when they drove towards the National Forest. "Only few people go up into the mountains and canyons[7]. Even though it's beautiful here all year round. In the wintertime you can go skiing and in the summertime it's much cooler and clearer than down at the coast."
They passed several pine-tree forests[8] and stopped at a lookout point with a view[9] over the Mojave Desert[10] in the East and San Fernando Valley in the West. "Two million people alone live down there," Justus said and pointed at huge residential areas[11]. Jimboy found the view of the desert even more impressive. One of the hottest deserts in the world, Bob explained. At the shore[12] of Lake Silverwood they suddenly stood in front of an ugly concrete[13] block. A long two-story building that looked like an army barrack or a prison camp for juvenile delin-

1 to crack: knacken
2 to inquire: nachforschen
3 to giggle: kichern
4 to volunteer: etwas freiwillig tun
5 graduation: Schulabschluss
6 boarding school: Internat
7 canyon: Schlucht
8 pine-tree forest: Pinienwald
9 view: Aussicht
10 desert: Wüste
11 residential area: Wohngebiet
12 shore: Ufer
13 concrete: Beton

quents[1]. On the left and right side of the main building there were cement walls. The main entrance[2] was blocked by a large security checkpoint.
"Awful," Justus thought. Jimboy's face also showed disappointment[3]. He looked from one to the other. Peter nodded at him encouragingly[4], "You have to like it from the inside, not from the outside. Besides, they must have their reasons for this kind of security."
"It is in a pretty lonely area," Bob agreed.
"Okay," said Jimboy, "just the first impression is ..."
He took his sports bag and determinedly[5] walked towards the entrance.
They saw several cameras above them. The entrance door of the security checkpoint opened as if by magic. It closed and locked behind them with a muffled thud[6]. There was nobody around. They walked into an empty foyer, which was the doorman's glass-paned[7] office. A huge[8] guy with a square face stood behind the window panes.
"What are your names?" he asked with a blank expression[9] on his face. Jimboy answered and introduced[10] the Three Investigators. "You guys can get lost[11]!" The man said. Peter stared at the guy. "What a blockhead[12]," he thought and just managed to swallow the insult[13].

1 juvenile delinquents: jugendliche Straftäter
2 entrance: Eingang
3 disappointment: Enttäuschung
4 encouragingly: ermunternd
5 determined: entschlossen
6 muffled thud: dumpfer Aufschlag
7 glass-paned: verglast
8 huge: riesig
9 blank expression on one's face: ausdruckslose Miene
10 to introduce someone: jmd. vorstellen
11 get lost!: haut ab!
12 blockhead: Holzkopf, Flegel
13 to swallow the insult: die Beleidigung „schlucken“

"We're not getting lost, we're accompanying[1] someone here," he explained instead of swearing[2].
"We wanted to bring our friend here and look at the boarding school," Justus said politely[3]. "That's not forbidden, is it?"
"It is," the doorman answered and pointed his thumb towards the sign on the wall behind him. 'Entrance for Authorized Persons only[4]' stood on the sign. "No exceptions[5]," he stressed[6] the point.
"Well, then," Justus said a bit too cheerfully and elbowed Jimboy's ribs. "You start your career – and we'll drive back home." When they walked out, they heard the man ask Jimboy to fill in several admission forms[7].
"I'm sure he'll quickly find a couple of friends," Peter said.
"Yeah, sure," Justus murmured. But he was happy that his job aspiration[8] at the moment was to be a lawyer and not a professional soccer player.

Detective question 2

Was meinst du dazu? Wer steckt hinter dem merkwürdigen Drohbrief?
Ist es nur ein böser Streich oder sollte man es ernstnehmen?

1 to accompany: begleiten
2 to swear: beschimpfen
3 polite: höflich
4 Authorized Persons only: nur Zugangsberechtigte
5 exception: Ausnahme
6 to stress something: etw. betonen
7 admission form: Anmeldeformular
8 job aspiration: Berufswunsch

3. Jimboy Momentarily Moans[1]

Bob's hands were quite calm when he stuck in the needle. He carefully scratched a small opening into the envelope, took the pincers and slowly put them through the hole. With one jerk[2] he tore off the thread to the fuse.

"Here, for you." In one movement he threw the letter to Peter who automatically opened his hands. He wanted to catch the letter and jerked back at the same time. The brown envelope sailed to the floor. "Very funny," he said.

Justus took out a handkerchief[3], bent over and carefully picked up the letter. They already searched the letter for finger-prints without success. Now he pulled out the contents[4]. One of those pages appeared. Peter looked over the First Investigator's shoulder and read aloud. "JIMBOY MOMENTARILY MOANS. JOGGERS CHASE[5] JEFFERSON."

"So we were right! This is about your cousin and those guys know that he is here!" Bob took the envelope from Justus and went to the trailer. "I'll take a look at the fuse mechanism."

Peter and Justus sat down on the old garden bench that Uncle Titus donated[6]. They exchanged their knowledge about Jefferson. The third president of the USA governed[7] the country in the early 1800's and founded[8] the Democratic Party. He was an exceptionally versatile[9] man, not only successful as a politician, but also as an architect and

1 to moan: jammern, stöhnen
2 jerk: Ruck
3 handkerchief: Taschentuch
4 contents: Inhalt
5 to chase: jagen
6 to donate: spenden
7 to govern: regieren
8 to found: gründen
9 exceptionally versatile: außergewöhnlich vielseitig

scientist. He also impressed his fellow citizens[1] because he was a talented musician, too.
"Maybe someone doubts our general educational background[2] and wants to test us," Justus joked[3]. "Or the whole thing is a joke," Peter said.
"I don't think so," they heard Bob's voice from the trailer. He appeared in the doorway. "The ingredients' mixture ratio was almost one to one this time," he said. "Enough to cause a couple of injured fingers. Or even worse. That's not a prankster[4]. He's a real criminal!"
Justus stood up. "Hand me the telephone number of the paper company."
"It's on the desk."
Justus went into the trailer. The two other boys heard him ask for a list of shops that sold the special kind of paper. Then he came back and joined both of them on the bench. "They'll send a fax."
"A good investment, that device[5]," the Second Investigator said.
Justus started to talk about the topic of money. "I haven't finished checking our balance sheets[6]. But I already know that we really have to lower our monthly costs."
"You talk like our mayor[7] when he's giving a speech about cost reduction for hospitals and kindergardens," Peter interrupted.
"With only one difference: I'm right," Justus answered. "Let's ask Uncle Titus to forget about the monthly fee[8] for the trailer site."
A bit later Justus held a list in his hand and reported that the paper stores were scattered[9] all over the whole area.

1 fellow citizen: Mitbürger(in)
2 general educational background: Allgemeinbildung
3 to joke: witzeln
4 prankster: Witzbold
5 device: Gerät
6 balance sheet: Bilanz
7 mayor: Bürgermeister(in)
8 fee: Gebühr
9 scattered: verstreut

They parked near two paper stores at the Rocky Beach town hall. But in both stores nobody had asked for the environmentally friendly[1] paper for a long time. Visiting the stores in Ventura and Oxnard didn't bring them any closer to a solution[2] either. They drove to downtown[3] Santa Monica. They had eleven addresses there, all of them in the elegant and bustling pedestrian[4] zone. Justus, who arrived at the meeting point in front of the department store 'Altman' first, felt frustrated. Some of the stores didn't sell that kind of paper at all and the others had regular customers[5]. Definitely too many regulars to check up on.

Bob and Peter came back. They hurried across the street. "We have a trace[6], maybe we're even on a really hot scent[7]," Bob cried out.

"Over there in a small shop," Peter said, "a salesperson remembered he sold the paper to a young man. It came from the warehouse[8] by mistake. The customer didn't really want it, but took it anyway[9]. Because otherwise he would have to wait again. But now the best part: Because of this mix-up[10] they even wrote down his address. The guy doesn't really live where he told them he did."

Justus knitted his brows[11]. "Where then? And you found out about all of this in a few minutes?"

"We didn't have to find out anything." The Second Investigator grinned. "Does the address '811 Horn Road' ring a bell[12]?"

"Stupid question. Our school."

1 environmentally friendly: umweltfreundlich
2 solution: Lösung
3 downtown: Stadtzentrum
4 pedestrian: Fußgänger
5 regular customer: Stammkunde
6 trace: Spur
7 hot scent: heiße Fährte
8 warehouse: Lagerhalle
9 anyway: trotzdem
10 mix-up: Verwechslung
11 to knit one's brows: Stirn runzeln
12 to ring a bell: bekannt vorkommen; klingelt es? *(Redewendung)*

"And an approximately twenty year old, dark-haired man doesn't live there, of course," Peter said and pulled his notebook out of the pocket of his pants. "... About my size and proportions and he wears a large gold chain around his neck."
"It's strange[1]," Justus said on the way home, "that somebody sends his hate mail on such extravagant paper, of all things."

Elizabeth got a digital camcorder as a present and became a real fan of making all kinds of films. "All kinds of possible and impossible films," Peter said when he wanted to tease[2] her. Actually he was proud of his girl-friend, who had a good feeling for the layout of pictures[3] and even mastered difficult pan-shots[4].
She couldn't stop thinking about what the Three Investigators told her – about the sports boarding school at Lake Silverwood. And so, instead of biking in the mountains they watched the soccer game nearby.

"Watch out, you can learn a lot," Kelly told the guys and turned on the video-recorder. "The team in black and white t-shirts is Smell's team," Elizabeth said.
"Now!" said Kelly. One of the Smell boys kicked the ball out of bounds[5].
"So what?" Bob asked and looked around without understanding. Justus and Peter preferred[6] to keep quiet and appear distinguished[7] They looked at the girls expectantly.
"You're not really watching. Open your eyes!" Elizabeth rewound the film, but even when they saw it the second time the three boys, who

1 strange: merkwürdig, fremd
2 to tease: ärgern, necken
3 layout of pictures: Bildaufteilung
4 pan-shot: Kameraschwenk
5 out of bounds: ins Aus
6 to prefer: bevorzugen
7 distinguished: vornehm

were normally such smart investigators, didn't notice anything unusual[1]. Even Justus, for once, didn't have an idea and just sat there silently with his arms folded and a frown[2] on his face. He couldn't stand it when other people were ahead of him. And he had the feeling that that was the case this time.

"Come on!" Peter said, "Don't you realize we can't see anything unusual?"

Kelly quietly said something that the three boys didn't understand. "Probably not a compliment," Justus thought. But then Kelly couldn't wait any longer.

"This guy here," she explained loudly, "who kicked the ball across the side line! He doesn't have any reason to do that! Nobody hassled[3] him, none of the opposing[4] forwards are nearby! Nothing, no reason whatsoever!"

"Aha," Peter said. The other two boys were silent.

The film showed more similar scenes. They always took place near the mid-line. After the third time that the ball was kicked out of bounds, Kelly focused on the boy who was picking up the ball. He took an unusually long time for the throw-in[5].

"That's not all," Kelly said, "the highlight is yet to come[6]." She filmed two collisions of Smell players: each time one of them ended up lying flat on the ground – and a really evil foul was committed behind the referee's back.

After that scene Elizabeth positioned herself in front of the TV. "I believe," she said, "that is, we believe, I mean, we're absolutely sure that the Smell team players interrupt[7] the game on purpose[8]."

1 unusual: ungewöhnlich
2 frown: herabgezogene Mundwinkel
3 to hassle: bedrängen
4 opposing: gegnerisch
5 throw-in: Einwurf
6 the highlight is yet to come: der Höhepunkt folgt noch
7 to interrupt: unterbrechen
8 on purpose: absichtlich

Peter looked sceptical. "For what reason?"
"That's just what you'll have to find out. You're the investigators!"
"Could the kick out of bounds be legal?" Justus grinned. "The rule book regulates the wildest things. In former times you could knock the goalkeeper off his feet or carry him off the playing-field, as long as he held the ball in his hands." The boys laughed, but the girls weren't in the mood[1] for laughing.
Jimboy's voice was on the answering machine. "I'm fine," he said briefly. "I'm playing in the school stadium in Glendale tomorrow afternoon. Come over if you can." Justus pinched his lower lip. His cousin didn't sound very happy. And the last sentence sounded strange. Almost like a cry for help.

The next day the boarding-school boys didn't play brilliantly. Jimboy wasn't as good as in Pasadena either. Again the ball was kicked out of bounds several times, again there were a few collisions between the eleven Smell team members. And besides, there were several fouls that were much too severe[2] for varsity league games, Peter thought.
"I'm sorry," Justus said after eighty minutes. "But I don't know much more than before."
Elizabeth shook her head and sent her hair flying. "This can't be true!" She called, "Are you guys blind?" And Kelly put her hands on her hips and looked at the Three Investigators fiercely[3]. "You just don't want to understand! You're just envious!"
After the final whistle Jimboy waved at them from afar and disappeared into the showers in a wooden building. A bus with an enormous, ugly, bright green logo on the side was standing in front of the building.

1 mood: Laune, Stimmung
2 severe: schwerwiegend
3 to look fierce: düster anfunkeln

“If the products taste as artificial[1] as that color – well then – enjoy your meal!” Bob shuddered[2].
“Certainly not,” Peter said. “Every day hundreds of thousands of customers buy and eat Smell products.”
“Not everything that hundreds of thousands of people do is … right.” Justus announced and looked at Peter and Bob to see if the sentence made an impression on them.
“Look over there, it’s Jimboy!” Kelly suddenly called. “He’s getting on the bus.”
“Hey, Jimboy! What’s going on[3]?” Justus called and ran towards the bus.
Jimboy appeared in the back door. “I didn’t see you,” he said and blushed[4]. “We have to leave right away.” He slowly walked down the three steps.
“How are you?” Justus asked. “How should I be?” His cousin answered stiffly. “Good.”
“And how’s the training camp?” Peter asked.
“Great. Really, absolutely great.”
“Get in, everybody get in!” A bossy[5] voice called from the inside of the bus. “That means you, too, Jonas.”
“I’ll call you.” Jimboy smiled a crooked[6] smile and got on the bus. Speechless, the five of them watched the bus leave.

12 “Can you tell us where we can find Mr Bow?” Justus asked the girl at the soft-drink booth[7].

1 artificial: künstlich
2 to shudder: sich schütteln, schaudern
3 what’s going on: was ist los
4 to blush: erröten
5 bossy: herrisch, im Kommandoton
6 crooked: schief, krumm
7 soft-drink booth: Getränkestand

"Over there at the beach, near the blue and white sunshades[1]," she answered with a friendly smile.
The Malibu Lagoon State Beach had quite a lot of visitors that day. "Any more and they'll be on top of each other," Justus thought. He climbed over four pairs of feet, and was blocked the next moment by a wall of bodies[2]. They were holding hands and dancing wildly. They were singing incomprehensible[3] tunes while dancing around. The sun was burning down on the sand. Big waves[4] were rolling in from the ocean.
A black-haired man sat at a round table underneath a sunshade. Next to him was a cash box[5] on one side and a chess board[6] on the other side. Facing him, sat a man wearing a large sun-hat. He reached towards one of the chess figures but then pulled his hand back again.
"We would like ...," Peter began to say."If you want sunshades or deck chairs[7], I'm sorry. I'm sold out. [8]" The man wearing sun-glasses pointed towards the crowded rows along the beach. The deck chairs were standing almost all the way down to the water.
"Actually not," the Second Investigator continued. "We want to talk to you."
"I have to leave anyway," The other man used this opportunity[9] to pull out a tray of roasted almonds[10] from underneath the table. "I'll be back in an hour," he said and suddenly he held an old post-horn

1 sunshade: Sonnenschirm
2 body: Körper
3 incomprehensible: unverständlich
4 wave: Welle
5 cash box: Kasse
6 chess board: Schachbrett
7 deck chair: Liegestuhl
8 sold out: ausverkauft
9 opportunity: Gelegenheit
10 roasted almonds: gebrannte Mandeln

in his hand. "Roasted almonds!" he yelled, then blew into the horn and marched off.
Justus took a look at the chess board. Mr Bow played the white figures and had one more castle[1] left over than his opponent.
"Eddy," Mr Bow grumbled, "A real character[2] here at the beach. Unfortunately he plays a lousy[3] game of chess. But, okay. What would you like to talk about?"
"If you are Mr Bow – about soccer," Bob said casually. Mr Bow raised his eyebrows.
"Mr Lloyd sent us," Justus explained.
The man's expression[4] became a bit friendlier. "Lloyd? He's still around?"
"Yes," Bob continued. "He works at the same newspaper as my dad and he told us that you could tell us all about the 'operation earphone'."
"The 'operation earphone'?" Bow opened his mouth and closed it again. Then he scrutinized[5] his visitors from top to bottom. "And why are you interested in those old stories, if I may ask?"
Justus didn't want him to know right away[6] that they were investigators. So he acted like an innocent[7] school-boy who was upset[8] because he got such explosive mail.
"If you want to hear the whole story, you'll have to be very patient," Bow said and the Three Investigators made themselves comfortable. Fortunately[9] Mr Bow was a good storyteller. But what he told them was exciting enough, anyway. He was a soccer referee in the seven-

1 castle: Turm im Schachspiel
2 a real character: Unikum
3 lousy: mies
4 expression: Ausdruck
5 to scrutinize: mustern
6 right away: sofort
7 innocent: unschuldig
8 upset: aufgebracht
9 fortunately: glücklicherweise

ties, first on the East coast and then in California. There was a story that almost landed him in prison. It started when some of the people who were in charge[1] at the National Soccer Association wanted to attract more customers for TV commercials in this sport.
"You must know," Bow said, "without commercial breaks, you can't sell a thing." Therefore they asked British experts to find out how to change the rules. They wanted to have regular breaks during a game so they could show commercials.
"Behind the scene another thing was going on," Mr Bow continued. Dubious[2] men who were working for important managers of a large trade association[3] talked to the CEO[4] of the referee-association[5]. They wanted to stay in the background and they asked if the game could be interrupted on purpose. Several referees, including Bow, got money for participating in secret tests. They called a penalty[6] that didn't really happen at the exact time when a commercial break should take place. And not only that. The men that stayed in the background pressured the bribed[7] referees. The official report[8] of the soccer association experts concluded that a change of rules didn't make sense because soccer would lose its typical character through regular commercial breaks.
"We were blackmailed[9]", Bow said. "They told us that they would reveal[10] the secret tests if we didn't play along." He stopped and seemed lost in thought for a moment. "We were stupid," he said then, "The men pulling the strings would have been caught[11] as well,

1 to be in charge: das Sagen haben
2 dubious: unseriös
3 trade association: Unternehmerverband
4 CEO: Abkürzung für chief executive officer: Geschäftsführer(in)
5 association: Vereinigung
6 penalty: Strafe, Strafstoß
7 bribed: bestochen
8 report: Gutachten
9 blackmailed: erpresst
10 to reveal: aufdecken, verraten
11 would have been caught: wären erwischt worden

if they had called[1] the police." But the referees didn't know each other. They couldn't discuss the problem with each other. They met in the witness stand of the courtroom[2], for the first time. They finally gave in because they were afraid of losing their licences and good reputation.

But before they could try out their evil scheme[3] the whole thing blew up in their faces – somebody squealed[4]. Bow and seven other referees got a ban[5] for life and, on top of that, they were sentenced to heavy fines[6] and 400 hours of social work.
"I was lucky," Bow ended. "I have a lease[7] on this nice piece of beach and mainly spend my time playing chess. There are worse things in life."
"Can you imagine that someone wants to play the same 'false game' again?" Peter asked.
"Hardly[8]," Bow waved his hand. "Nowadays spectators[9] can watch a game on the large screen even more close-up than in former times. There are slow-motion-repeat sequences[10]. And surely you also know that they are thinking about using video as proof[11]. Just like ice-hockey. A referee has to watch a sequence on a TV screen at the side of the ice-hockey rink before he decides about a penalty[12]. They would suspect[13] him right away if he constantly said something else than what

1 if they had called: wenn sie angerufen hätten
2 witness stand of the courtroom: Zeugenstand im Gerichtssaal
3 scheme: Plan, Komplott
4 to squeal: verpfeifen
5 ban: Berufsverbot
6 sentenced to fines: zu Geldstrafen verurteilt
7 lease: Pacht
8 hardly: kaum
9 spectator: Zuschauer(in)
10 slow-motion-repeat sequences: Wiederholung in Zeitlupe
11 proof: Beweis
12 penalty: Strafe
13 to suspect someone: jmd. verdächtigen

the video shows." He shook his head. "No, I believe nowadays you have to use a different method."
The First Investigator listened attentively[1]. "And which method? Maybe secretly co-operating[2] with the players?"
"You are tough[3], aren't you?" Bow smiled. "I can imagine a lot of things the older I get." Then he turned back to his chess board without saying anything else.

Again the investment[4] in a fax machine paid off[5]. Bob asked his father for help one more time. Now his father sent them whatever he found in the newspaper's archive about the company Smell, page by page. A French immigrant by the name of Victor Sentir founded the company in New Orleans at the beginning of the century[6]. He soon opened a branch in Denver, where they cultivate sugar-beets[7] at the foot of the Rocky Mountains. Later, there were also meat factories in Dallas and Chicago, peanut plantations in Georgia, a cooking oil refinery[8] in Houston, canneries[9] in California and two mills[10] near Niagara Falls. The variety of products ranged from canned milk[11] and peanut butter to sausages, bread and sugar. After the Second World War Sentir's heirs[12] opened up a huge chain[13] which also had branches in Japan and South America. They sold preserves[14] and frozen food. The young-

1 attentive: aufmerksam
2 to co-operate: zusammenarbeiten, kooperieren
3 tough: zäh
4 investment: Investition
5 to pay off: bezahlt machen, rentieren
6 century: Jahrhundert
7 sugar-beet: Zuckerrübe
8 refinery: Raffinerie
9 cannery: Konservenfabrik
10 mill: Mühle
11 canned milk: Dosenmilch
12 heir: Erbe
13 chain: Kette
14 preserves: Konserven

est son became one of the many wine-makers near San Francisco. He was also the one who started the sports sponsoring.
Many small grocery stores[1] couldn't compete[2] with the cheap prices and the fine product quality that the discounter Smell offered[3]. They had to sell their stores – to Smell. That's how the enterprise expanded to a chain of stores by the name of 'Shooter' with many branches at choice locations[4]. Often the former owners[5] didn't have any other alternative – they had to sign a leasing contract if they wanted to survive somehow. So they became the leaseholders[6]. The farmers also had strict contracts with Smell. They promised to buy large amounts of peanuts, sugar, beef or grain. In return, the farmers guaranteed that they would not raise the prices for five years, whether they had good or bad harvests[7].
Peter shook his head and threw the documents on the table. The case was clear: Whoever couldn't fulfill the contract faced ruin.
"That is such a dirty trick," he said.
"Something like that should be illegal," Bob ranted[8] "I wouldn't be surprised if they treated[9] their athletes the same way."

Detective question 3

Wieso verhält Jimboy sich so seltsam? Glaubst du, er fühlt sich wohl im Internat und in seiner Fußballmannschaft? Was lernen die Jungs dort – außer Fußballspielen?

1 grocery store: Lebensmittelladen
2 to compete: in Wettbewerb treten
3 to offer: anbieten
4 choice location: bevorzugte Lage
5 former owner: ehmalige(r) Besitzer(in)
6 leaseholder: Pächter(in)
7 harvest: Ernte
8 to rant: schimpfen, meckern
9 to treat: behandeln

4. A Trip To The Lake

They visited the few residential areas around the Lake looking for 'Shooter' stores. There were two stores in Crestline. A gas station attendant[1] told them that Larry Wilcox, one of the lease holders, delivered groceries to the boarding school every day. "He always arrives in the afternoon around five o'clock," the talkative[2] man at the gas station said, "and he returns about an hour later." The Shooter branch was near a few small art galleries in pretty buildings with brick fronts. 'Delivery Entrance[3]' was written on the sign. A few yards further on they arrived at a warehouse. When they passed by, Justus peered into one of the barred[4] windows. They found what they were looking for behind the warehouse: obviously someone was just loading a truck. The truck's double door was wide open. They walked around as inconspicuously[5] as possible. There was nobody around. Without speaking, the First Investigator pointed at the loading platform that was half-way unloaded.

"Watch out!" Bob hissed and pulled his friends behind a pile of boxes that was man-high.

Footsteps were coming closer. "... with Sally and the children," said a deep voice. "I just love barbecues." Two employees in white coats carried boxes full of groceries to the truck and passed close by the Three Investigators.

Justus pulled in his neck. The footsteps moved away again. "Stay here!" he whispered[6]. Taking big steps he went to the loading space[7] and took a look at the groceries. 'Smell Silverwood' was written on

1 gas station attendant: Tankwart
2 talkative: gesprächig
3 delivery entrance: Liefereingang
4 barred: vergittert
5 inconspicuous: unauffällig
6 to whisper: flüstern
7 loading space: Ladefläche

a pile of cans. “Here we go,” he said satisfied[1]. He waved to the other two boys and a few seconds later the trio sat in the loading space hidden[2] behind boxes. The ride barely took a quarter of an hour. Then they heard someone open the door. Right after that, light shone into the delivery van. The van started to rock[3] when someone – probably Larry – jumped on the loading platform. The Three Investigators held their breath[4]. They would be caught in a tight space[5] if Larry unloaded the boxes first. Justus clenched[6] his fists. They heard a shuffling sound[7], then a groan[8] and then the van rocked again.

“It’s me. Larry,” a voice said. They heard footsteps walking away. Justus murmured something about only the brave being lucky[9]. The first hurdle[10] was taken. Justus peered[11] outside. “Nobody is around, let’s go,” he said. He jumped out of the van[12] and ran to the building for momentary cover[13]. He had to grin when he looked down at his sneakers[14] and track-suit bottoms[15]. The three boys had dressed up[16] in real sports outfits so nobody recognized that they were strangers[17] right away. Justus pulled in his belly and walked quickly toward the administration building[18]. He opened a wide swinging door.

1 satisfied: zufrieden
2 hidden: versteckt
3 to rock: schaukeln
4 to hold one’s breath: Atem anhalten
5 to be caught in a tight space: eng werden *(Redewendung)*
6 to clench: ballen, anspannen
7 shuffling sound: schlurfendes Geräusch
8 to groan: stöhnen
9 only the brave are lucky: wer wagt, gewinnt *(Redewendung)*
10 hurdle: Hürde
11 to peer: spähen, blicken
12 van: Lieferwagen
13 momentary cover: vorübergehende Deckung
14 sneakers: Turnschuhe
15 track-suit bottoms: Trainingshose
16 to dress up: sich verkleiden
17 strangers: Fremde
18 administration building: Verwaltungsgebäude

A group of boys approached them. "Hi," he said when they passed each other. His heart was beating[1] wildly. Two or three of the boys reacted and also greeted[2] them, but nobody really paid attention to them. The athletes were deeply involved in a discussion about the sense[3] of a training unit[4] that only allowed kicking through passes[5].
Justus looked around the hallway. A lot of teachers and trainers had their offices here. Most doors had signs with their names and functions. Everything was quiet. Justus climbed up one flight of stairs[6]. 'Gary Coranado, sports/stamina coach[7]' was written on the first door and on the left was Mike Hammer's office, who was responsible for soccer/tactics. Justus squatted[8] down and looked through the keyhole into Mr Hammer's office. There wasn't a sound. Carefully he gripped[9] the doorknob.
At the same moment, a door opened a few yards away. Sunlight shone into the hallway. First a blue pants[10] leg appeared. It belonged to a man wearing a bright red sweater.
"Good afternoon, Sir," Justus said firmly[11].
"Hello," the man answered briefly and came towards him. He frowned. "Who are you?"
"Jonas," Justus answered and wasn't even lying[12]. "I'm new here."
"And what are you looking for?" the man asked. He stopped directly in front of him.

1 to beat: schlagen
2 to greet: grüßen
3 sense: Sinn
4 training unit: Trainingseinheit
5 through pass: Steilpass
6 flight of stairs: eine Treppe
7 stamina: Kondition
8 to squat: hocken
9 to grip: greifen
10 pants (US): Hose
11 firm: fest – *hier*: mit fester Stimme
12 to lie: lügen

"Abe Courthouse's office." Of course the First Investigator's mastermind memorized all of the names that he read on the doors so far. A Mr Abe Courthouse, math teacher, existed at this strange[1] institution.
"I've got a problem with the math books that we used at the school in Chicago."
"One floor[2] down. Third door from the exit, on the right."
"Thank you, Sir."
Justus stood still. The man stayed as well. "Anything else?"
"Yes, Sir ... is there a restroom[3] for students?"
"At the foot of the stairs." The man pointed in the direction that Justus just[4] came from.

15 Peter wasn't so interested in the field tracks[5] where several students were running laps. He was attracted to[6] the locations where the tactics practice[7] was going on. Hidden behind a row of bushes he carefully walked closer to a circle of eight boys that were standing around their coach.
"The corner also offers," he heard the blond man in the center say, "a suitable opportunity[8]. The ball's in the off, you have time to get it. And then you take a lot of time to prepare yourself." Then he spoke about the different corner ball variations, with momentum[9] towards the goal, with momentum away from the goal towards a team mate, towards the goal post[10] nearer to the ball, towards the goal post further away from the ball and as a short pass to a team mate.

1 strange: seltsam
2 floor: Stockwerk
3 restroom: Toilette
4 just: gerade eben, nur
5 field tracks: Leichtathletikbahn
6 attracted to: angezogen von
7 practice: Training
8 suitable opportunity: passende Gelegenheit
9 momentum: Drall, Effet
10 goal post: Torpfosten

Carefully keeping his cover, Peter tiptoed[1] to one of the small wooden huts at the side of the playing field. "Today I want to work on the worst[2] of all corner variations," he heard the coach saying, "... when the opposing team's defense[3] gets the ball." The Second Investigator decided not to listen to the good advice[4] for this quite unpleasant[5] case and ran through the half-open door.

Surprised he looked around. He expected a room with balls, nets, clubs or hoops[6] for technique coaching.

Actually he stood inside a fully equipped office that was like their trailer in Rocky Beach. There was a TV set, a video recorder and a computer. On the inside the wooden shed[7] had firm brick[8] walls with barred windows and a safety lock[9] at the door. A huge picture was hanging on the wall opposite[10] the door. A dozen sweating[11] men waving and laughing, were posing for the camera. His eyes wandered from the picture of the Brazilian world champions to the desk and the bunch of keys on top of it. Determined, he picked it up, took down the picture and found what he expected: a small gray metal box with two locks. The shortest key fit the top lock but none of the keys fit into the bottom[12] lock. Peter pulled his own little box of equipment out of his pants, opened the case and grabbed the appropriate tool[13] without hesitating. The safe opened with a low popping sound. It

1 to tiptoe: auf Zehenspitzen gehen, schleichen
2 worst: schlimmste
3 defense: Verteidigung
4 advice: Ratschlag
5 quite unpleasant: ziemlich unerfreulich
6 clubs or hoops: Keulen oder Reifen
7 shed: Hütte
8 brick: Ziegelstein
9 safety lock: Sicherheitsschloss
10 opposite: gegenüber
11 sweating: schwitzend
12 bottom: unteres
13 appropriate tool: passendes Werkzeug

was empty except for a DVD. Peter hesitated for a second, then he put the DVD into his pocket and locked the safe again.

In his hide-away[1] behind the large dishwasher Bob listened to a few trivial conversations. In the morning, one of the kitchen-helpers injured his hand so badly cutting vegetables that they had to take him to the hospital. When Larry came in with his grocery delivery[2] the conversation turned to more interesting topics. The two men started to talk about cheating[3] at ball games. One of the men said that twenty years ago the 'Diego Rams' bought a player, a defender. He pretended to disturb[4] the opponents' game.

"It would have been[5] ok – if Franky hadn't squealed," the voice said.

"When you cheat, it's the same as playing a good game," Larry said, "It all depends on practise. Short cigarette break[6]?" The other man agreed and, to Bob's annoyance[7], they left the kitchen.

He ran to a window where he could watch the van. The van was almost empty. But now, several boxes with empty bottles were on the loading platform.

"Calling scout[8] number one and two. Please come in," Bob whispered into his walkie-talkie. "The taxi is ready to leave."

16 "You really had a sixth sense[9]," Justus said. "I admit[10] it all seemed very unrealistic. But these scenes are proof enough." The DVD that Peter stole at the training camp showed six different game situations

1 hide-away: Versteck
2 grocery delivery: Lieferung von Lebensmittel
3 to cheat: betrügen
4 to disturb: stören
5 would have been – wäre gewesen
6 break: Pause
7 annoyance: Ärger
8 scout: Späher(in)
9 sixth sense: übernatürlicher Sinn, sechster/siebter Sinn
10 to admit: zugeben

in extreme slow-motion. And they all had one thing in common[1]: they used the situations to interrupt a soccer match on purpose. Either by using fouls – one time a player elbowed another player, aiming[2] exactly at his kidneys[3], and was hidden from view by his own body – or by a harmless[4] but spectacular looking collision with a team mate. The end of the scene was always the same – exactly like the game that the girls watched and filmed a few days ago: Somebody was rolling on the ground and the next break occurred[5].

Justus reported that he had called Jimboy on the phone when they got back. He said very little and only revealed one secret: After a couple of days three boys already quit Smell camp. Now they were looking for other players. The next day they planned to have another try-out[6] in Ventura.

Peter didn't hesitate[7]. "I'll go there. If I'm lucky they'll take me."

Elizabeth couldn't resist[8] teasing him. "You're lucky that you got the DVD. If you still hadn't believed us we could have started another detective agency."

Lys giggled. "We already have a name for it."

"The Three !!!," Kelly and Elizabeth called out in one voice[9].

It was the seventeenth minute of the try-out game. The sports managers of the food manufacturer scheduled[10] it as the last game. It started to drizzle[11] and the fine rain made the lawn as slippery[12] as a

1 in common: gemeinsam haben
2 to aim: zielen
3 kidney: Niere
4 harmless: harmlos
5 to occur: passieren, geschehen
6 try-out: Testspiel
7 to hesitate: zögern
8 to resist: widerstehen
9 in one voice: wie aus einem Mund
10 to schedule: Termin ansetzen
11 to drizzle: nieseln
12 slippery: rutschig

wet bar of soap[1]. One team mate kicked a cross from the right side in front of the goal. Peter took the ball in the air using an incredible bicycle kick[2]. The ball touched down inside the goal and the kicker landed painfully on his behind[3]. When he wanted to get up, you could see the pain on his face. Peter grabbed his knee. Justus, who stood next to Bob behind the fence, knew immediately what that meant: a stretcher and a hospital room again. Justus thumped his friend's shoulder encouragingly but couldn't think of any other comment than: "Your bicycle kick was terrific!" Then the doctor arrived. And he came to the point right away. A torn cruciate ligament, hospital, leg in a plaster cast[4], crutches. And a young female doctor told him to go easy on his knee by sitting down and bedding his leg on pillows. Feeling depressed they drove to the home of the Shaw family. They lived in a small residential area in a pine forest on the outskirts[5] of Rocky Beach. Peter's mother was waiting with a freshly-baked cherry pie.

"You're lucky that you didn't have to stay at the hospital," she consoled[6] him while they were drinking coffee, because Peter's mood was simply not improving[7].

"But I wanted to ...," Peter started to say.

"... be in the finals, I know, " his mother interrupted him. "That will have to wait one more year. "

1 bar of soap: Seifenstück
2 bicycle kick: Fallrückzieher
3 behind: Hinterteil
4 plaster cast: Gips
5 outskirts: Außenbezirk, Stadtrand
6 to console: besänftigen, trösten
7 to improve: verbessern

Peter sighed[1]. Then he winked at his friends and got up clumsily[2]. He limped[3] ahead of them to his room leaning on crutches[4]. "What now?" he asked sadly after he made himself comfortable on his couch.
"Now you will do what you always wanted to do," Justus answered. "You will finally read all of Raymond Chandler's crime stories in one go[5]."
Peter made a face. "And what are you going to do?"
"We will draw straws: who tackles the next tasks[6]," said Justus. The door opened and Peter's mother told Justus: "Your uncle called. A man was searching for you. He didn't leave his name. But he left an envelope for you."

Detective question 4

Was geht vor in dem Internat am See?
Welchem Geheimnis kommt Peter im Trainingsgelände auf die Spur?

1 to sigh: seufzen
2 clumsy: ungeschickt
3 to limp: humpeln
4 crutches: Krücken
5 in one go: auf ein Mal, in einem Rutsch
6 to tackle a task: die Aufgabe angehen

5. On a Hot Scent

"He did seem a bit nervous," Uncle Titus said when he gave Bob the brown envelope. At first it didn't look like one of the mysterious letters.
"Go on! Was he tall or short? What color was his hair?" Justus urged[1] his uncle.
"I was just stacking up[2] the old ceramic pipes over there." Uncle Titus pointed to the dirty-yellow pile beside the garage. "That's why I didn't take a closer look at him. Besides[3], he said that you knew what it's about."
"This letter is much heavier than the others," Bob said when they arrived at the trailer. "And it's a different kind[4] of envelope."
"This certainly isn't a stink bomb," Justus said. He was right. Bob worked just as carefully as on the last hate mail. But there was neither a thread nor[5] a mechanism, instead there were twenty pages of paper that were covered in fine print[6].
"From Bow!" Justus called out surprised when he took a look at the letter. "Bow was here!"
"Great," said Bob. "That saves[7] you a trip to Malibu."
They bent over the papers. The former referee told them that he searched through his old stuff[8] after their conversation. He found the verdict[9] and the records of his lawsuit[10]. "Read for yourself," was

1 to urge: drängen
2 to stack up: aufstapeln
3 besides: außerdem
4 kind: Art
5 neither … nor: weder … noch
6 fine print: kleingedruckt
7 to save: ersparen, retten
8 stuff: Zeug
9 verdict: Urteil
10 lawsuit: Prozess

handwritten there. "Especially page 12 will interest you." Bow wrote that he unfortunately[1] forgot that, in the past, players were also involved. Justus started to read from the beginning of the letter again. Bob reached for page number 12. "That is crazy!" he whispered after reading it, but Justus only answered "Shhh!". He was reading with growing excitement: about a sweeper who testified in court[2] that he was offered a special kind of coaching. But nobody asked about the meaning of that at the time – it was only about the referees' wrongdoings[3]. Bow also wrote down the name of the witness[4]: a certain Mike Hammer.

"Can you imagine, Bow contacted us!" Bob ran into Peter's room. He was still resting[5] on the couch and watching TV.
"Can you imagine the TV channel ITN TV are in cahoots[6] with Smell!" he answered with the same excited tone of voice.
"What?" Bob opened his eyes wide.
"Not everybody at the same time!" Justus commanded[7]. "First our patient!" Then Peter reported that he spent the last two hours watching the TV recording[8] of a European Champions League match. "Every ten minutes there was a commercial break. Of course, not a problem when you're watching a recording. But if it's a live broadcast[9] everything is different, as you know. If we assume our suspicion[10] is correct, then Smell not only needs the players that play along – but also a

1 unfortunately: leider
2 to testify in court: bei Gericht aussagen
3 wrongdoing: Vergehen, Missetaten
4 witness: Zeuge
5 to rest: ausruhen
6 in cahoots: unter einer Decke stecken
7 to command: befehlen
8 recording: Aufzeichnung
9 broadcast: Sendung, Ausstrahlung
10 we assume our suspicion is correct: wir nehmen an, unser Verdacht

partner at the broadcasting station who presses the right button at the right moment."

Justus stared at the TV screen where a commercial was showing. For once[1], he scratched his head instead of pinching his lip. "But when is the correct moment?" he thought aloud. "Somehow the bribed players are informed about the exact time to get started… right when the next commercial break is about to[2] start. That's not an easy thing to do during[3] a live broadcast."

Bob took a TV magazine from Peter's desk. "Tomorrow afternoon there is a live broadcast of the Champions League Final. That would be a good opportunity to watch how the commercial breaks work[4] there."

"I'll do that," Peter suggested[5]. "And what is going on with Bow?"

"He gave us an interesting tip," Bob answered and gave them a brief report.

"Do you know anything else about this Mr Hammer, except that he's probably a teacher who coaches soccer and tactics for Smell nowadays[6]?"Peter finally wanted to know. Then he pulled out a dumbbell[7] from behind some big, bright pillows and murmured something about "A rolling stone gathers no moss[8]" and started to rhythmically push the heavy thing into the air.

Justus was imagining the man wearing a red sweater in front of him, who almost spoilt[9] everything. With closed eyes he searched his famous mastermind memory. Something that he saw in Hammer's

1 for once: ausnahmsweise
2 about to: kurz davor
3 during: während
4 to work: funktionieren, arbeiten
5 to suggest: vorschlagen
6 nowadays: heutzutage
7 dumbbell: Hantel
8 a rolling stone gathers no moss: Wer rastet, der rostet. *(Redewendung)*
9 to spoil: verderben

office bothered[1] him. "There was an emblem with black stripes. Something was written underneath it." Justus opened his eyes for a moment then quickly shut them again. "Exactly: San Diego Hotspurs." He looked at his watch, jumped up and ran out of the room.
Peter sat up. "If the Hammer that Bow met was also a Hotspurs center forward – then we've made a lot of progress."
"Larry also talked about a club from San Diego, the Rams. But I actually thought they were football players."
The door suddenly flew open. "I called Jimboy," Justus said before his friends could ask.
"And ...?"
"They always have time off[2] between training and lunch. I actually got a hold[3] of him. I wanted him to help us find out everything about Mike Hammer." He pulled a face. "He won't do it. Instead, he told me there was quite a lot of excitement because of a stolen DVD. If they only knew ...!"

18 The next day they tried in vain[4] to contact Bow or Lloyd in order to ask them about Mike Hammer. One man didn't have a phone at his beach house and the other one was on a trip to Canada with friends for a few days.
So they went to ITN TV. Bob's father gave them the name of a friend from university who was the head of the sports department at this TV station. Quite a lot of interested visitors[5] were standing at the main entrance. They were waiting for a guided[6] tour to start. Justus and Bob joined them and passed the security checkpoint without any problems. Justus was fascinated when he saw the high, empty studios

1 to bother: stören
2 time off: Freizeit
3 to get a hold of someone: jmd. erwischen
4 in vain: umsonst
5 visitor: Besucher(in)
6 guided: geführt

and so many spotlights on the ceiling[1]. At this time of the day there was already a lot going on. Documentaries, commercials and soaps[2] were produced here, as well as news and sports broadcasts.

The female student that guided them couldn't – or wasn't allowed to – give anything but standard answers. "But she's got great blond curls[3]," Bob mocked[4]. His question about the amount of time for commercials in ITN TV's programme only made the young lady frown.

When they arrived at the little French coffee shop after the guided tour, Eric Randolph was already waiting for them. He was a nice man in his mid-forties with an athletic figure and short gray, curly hair. Justus explained that they wanted to talk to him because they were worried[5] about Jimboy. "This sports boarding school seems to be quite strange," the First Investigator told the journalist while Bob organized ice tea.

They sat down at a round table with a view over the whole place. Randolph told them that there were more than forty sports boarding schools all over the continent. They were financed by Smell. They didn't house soccer players in most boarding schools. Only track and field[6] athletes, surfers, sailors and in one school even skiers. "The drill is tough," Randolph confirmed, "But for many athletes it's worth it. Smell is a real talent-factory. The same as being in a famous club in former times. Whoever successfully finishes one of these boarding schools has a fair market value[7]."

Justus told him about his cousin's quick employment and then cleverly turned[8] the conversation to the topic of Mike Hammer. At first Ran-

1 spotlights on the ceiling: Scheinwerfer an der Decke
2 soap, *abbreviation for soap-opera*: Seifenoper, Serie
3 curls: Locken
4 to mock: sich mokieren, spotten
5 to worry: sich Sorgen machen
6 track and field: Leichtathletik
7 market value: Marktwert
8 to turn to: lenken auf

dolph didn't associate[1] anything on hearing the name. Then Bob mentioned the San Diego Hotspurs.
"They don't exist anymore. They haven't for a long time," the sports journalist said. "They didn't survive[2] the first soccer boom, like a lot of other clubs." He thought about it. "They produced an excellent player." He frowned. "Possibly his name was Hammer. I'll ask at the archive." He dialled[3] four numbers on his cell phone[4], but nobody answered the phone. "Call me again in the afternoon," he said in a friendly tone. "By then I'll have the facts."
He wanted to stand up. "I have one more question," Bob said quickly.
"Shoot!" The man sunk back into his chair.
"I'm working part-time at a concert agency," Bob started to say. "And at the moment they are considering[5] whether TV commercials are an option for them or not... especially during sports broadcasts. My boss would love to place TV commercials at certain times on short notice[6], for example if an event isn't sold out yet. Which kind of sports would be suitable?"
Randolph mentioned a number of different kinds of sports. He didn't include[7] soccer, though[8].
"And soccer?" Justus asked innocently.
The man hesitated briefly. "That will depend on the experiences with the professional league," he said with a deadpan[9] expression. "So, but now I have to leave." He stood up. "The ice tea is on me[10]."

1 to associate: verbinden mit, assozieren
2 to survive: überleben
3 to dial: wählen
4 cell phone (US): Handy
5 to consider: erwägen, bedenken
6 on short notice: kurzfristig
7 to include: einschließen
8 though: jedoch
9 deadpan: ausdruckslos
10 on me: auf meine Rechnung

Detective question 5

Was sendet der hilfsbereite Mr Bow mit der Post? Noch einen explosiven Drohbrief?

6. Mr Bow Knows Nothing

Attentively Justus looked in the side mirror[1] of the car. He hesitated. The next moment he quietly whistled through his teeth. "You know what? Someone is following[2] us."

"Following? Us?"

Without moving his head Bob took a quick look in the rear view mirror[3]. "That small blue Ford in the right lane[4], three cars behind us. It was also in front of ITN TV. Besides, he wanted to turn north just now and he changed his mind[5] all of a sudden." The First Investigator looked straight ahead again. "That is too much coincidence[6]. Exit at Lincoln Boulevard! Then we'll see what happens."

Bob signalled a right turn[7] and drove towards the next exit leading off[8] the freeway. "What now?" Bob asked.

"Towards the Santa Monica Mountains!" Justus looked in the mirror again. "Loyal company[9]. And loyalty must be rewarded." He searched for the camera in the glove compartment[10], held it towards the back and pressed the release button[11].

They were in a high-class neighbourhood of Los Angeles. Many famous actors[12] and film directors[13] had their mansions[14] here. Bob

1 side mirror: Seitenspiegel
2 to follow: verfolgen
3 rear view mirror: Rückspiegel
4 lane: Fahrspur
5 to change one's mind: die Meinung ändern
6 coincidence: Zufall
7 signalled a right turn: blinken, um rechts abzubiegen
8 to lead off: wegführen
9 loyal company: anhängliche Begleitung
10 glove compartment: Handschuhfach
11 release button: Auslöser
12 actor: Schauspieler
13 film director: Regisseur(in)
14 mansion: Villa

knew his way around pretty well because Elizabeth liked to drive around in this area. She couldn't get enough of[1] looking at the unusual architecture of the houses.
"Hold on!" Bob called sharply turning the steering wheel[2] and drove into a small side street. He made a fast turn with the sound of screeching tires[3] and a few seconds later he stood in the direction of the flowing traffic[4] again. But the blue Ford that he wanted to pursue[5] didn't show up[6]. The two boys looked at each other confused. "That can't be true," Bob gnashed his teeth[7]. "He disappeared into thin air."

Bob printed the photographs of their pursuer[8]. "It's a woman!" he called excitedly. In fact the silhouette of a person with long hair could be seen. "Men don't have curls like that," Bob stated with the air of an expert[9].
Just then Justus noticed that the license plate[10] was out of focus[11]. "Is that the best print?" he asked his friend. Bob looked at him moodily[12]. "Do you think I create picture puzzles on purpose?"
Justus said something unintelligible[13] and looked at the photograph again. The only thing that was sure was that it was a California license plate. It wasn't clear if the first number on the license plate was a three or an eight, the second number a one or a seven and the forth

1 to get enough of: genug kriegen
2 steering wheel: Lenkrad
3 screeching tires: quietschende Reifen
4 flowing traffic: fließender Autoverkehr
5 to pursue: verfolgen
6 to show up: auftauchen
7 to gnash one's teeth: Zähne knirschen
8 pursuer: Verfolger(in)
9 air of an expert: Kennermiene
10 license plate: Nummernschild
11 out of focus: unscharf
12 moodily: launisch
13 unintelligible: unverständlich

number a zero or a nine. He went into the office, sat down at the desk and started to write down all kinds of variations on this license plate. Then he sent an e-mail to police inspector Cotta who was a friend at the Rocky Beach police force.

20 Ten minutes later they were already stuck in a gigantic traffic jam[1] again, slowly driving along the coastal route towards Los Angeles.
"A few days ago your father's newspaper wrote that 40 percent of the people living here think that cars ruin their city," Justus announced.
Bob nodded his head. "I also read that. But a good 20 percent didn't even take the bus once during the past ten years."
Half a mile before the Lagoon State Beach Bob parked his VW-beetle between two long Chevies[2]. Then they jogged across the sand. Mr Bow's blue and white sunshades appeared on the crowded[3] beach. Suddenly Bob pulled Justus behind a wicker beach chair[4] and nodded his head towards Bow who was straight ahead at his cashier's[5] table. Justus focused on the man at Bow's side and recognized[6] him. It was Eric Randolph. The gray-haired head of the sports department[7] was talking with the former referee. Then they shook hands and Randolph left. When they arrived at the table Bow turned his back towards them.
"Hello," Bob said. Bow quickly turned around but kept his left hand behind his back and stuffed[8] something into the back pocket of his pants. "Money," Justus suddenly thought, "Randolph gave him money. And how strange – the way he quickly flops into his chair."

1 traffic jam: Verkehrsstau
2 Chevie: *abbreviation for* Chevrolet (amerik. Automarke)
3 crowded: überfüllt
4 wicker beach chair: Strandkorb
5 cashier: Kassierer
6 to recognize: erkennen
7 head of department: Leiter der Abteilung
8 to stuff: stopfen

"Oh, it's you." Bow's greeting[1] didn't sound exactly enthusiastic.
"Thanks for the material," Justus began. "We have a couple more questions."
"But I probably can't give you any answers." Bow's face had a reserved expression.
"How do you know, since we haven't asked yet?"
Bow looked from one to the other. Then he pulled back his shoulders. He seemed to realize that he had made a mistake. "I slept terribly last night," he mumbled.
Justus decided on a surprise attack[2]. "What do you know about Mike Hammer?"
"Mike Hammer?" For a moment Bow acted as if he never heard the name before. Then he changed his mind. "Oh, him... you mean the witness from back then." Bow scratched his head for a long time. "I don't know anything about Mike Hammer."
"And what about Franky?" Bob asked abruptly. Justus looked at his friend surprised. "Franky, from the 'Rams'?" Bob stared at Bow who opened his eyes wide but was in control again immediately. "That was quite a good club," he said casually.
"And that affair[3]?"
"Affair?" Bow echoed. "I know nothing about an affair." He stood up leaning on the small table. "And now I have work to do." He started to sort pieces of paper that were underneath the small green cash box. "Money doesn't grow on trees," he said. "If I remember anything else, I'll contact you."
Justus stood there and pinched his lower lip. Bow's behaviour[4] was very strange. Why did he tell them so much the first time they came here and why did he, to top that off, send them twenty pages of information even though he was obviously involved in the case him-

1 greeting: Begrüßung
2 surprise attack: Überraschungsangriff
3 affair: Affäre
4 behaviour: Verhalten

self? "People are sometimes incomprehensible," Justus thought and felt a bit like a philosopher. Then he remembered that he read about people who are attracted to danger – they like to play with fire.
The beep from Bob's pants pocket stopped Justus' profound[1] thoughts. Bob walked out of ear-shot[2] and opened the small cell phone. "Yes, ... this is Bob speaking," he said briefly. He listened for a few seconds and blushed a bit. He said nothing except "Oh!" and finally, "We'll be there soon." He closed the cell phone. "That was Peter. The girls solved our case."

21 They sat down at a big round table and Peter pushed a stool underneath his leg that was still in a cast. Then Lys told them about the discovery[3] that they'd made at the school party the day before – she did this as matter-of-factly as possible because she didn't want to annoy[4] Justus any more than necessary. One of the female cooks, who prepared lunch at the school canteen every day, introduced them to her nephew[5], Tony, who was visiting. They thought he was quite nice and went for a walk around the school with him. And then he started to complain[6] about soccer. "We spurred him on[7]," Lys said. "Just for fun, of course."
Suddenly Tony was swearing like a trooper[8], about soccer stars such as Cobi Jones and Alexi Lalas who wanted to 'steal' away the traditional sports from the Americans. He criticized[9] several Brazilians and this dreadful Italian, Roberto Baggio and a certain German named

1 profound: tiefgründig
2 out of ear-shot: außer Hörweite
3 discovery: Entdeckung
4 to annoy: verärgern, nerven
5 nephew: Neffe
6 to complain about: sich beschweren über
7 to spur on: antreiben
8 to swear like a trooper: schimpfen wie ein Rohrspatz
9 criticize: kritisieren

Jürgen Klinsmann. Finally he totally blew his lid[1] and stormed off as if running after an invisible opponent.
"I followed him," Kelly continued. "Actually I wanted to calm him down. He was really nice." But then she saw him meet one of the boys who watched Jimboy's first performance as a soccer player. "Ronald Bush, you know, that loudmouth[2]," Kelly said. Peter nodded. He already forgot about his anger[3], he was even almost a bit proud of his girlfriend now. Lys had the best idea after all[4]. She asked about Ronald's exam results[5] in the past school term. She heard that one of the literature lectures[6] was about alliterations. Then she even secretly broke into the classroom where the tests were kept. And she found a text interpretation about the Myth of the Nibelungs.
"About Siegfried and his bath in the blood of the dragon, named Fafnir," Justus interrupted and got some dirty looks because he just couldn't keep his trap[7] shut. Then Elizabeth told them excitedly[8] how they confronted the two suspects[9] with her conclusions. "After a few minutes the whole thing was clear. Ronald and Tony argued[10] and accused[11] each other and that's how they delivered the final proof."
"What a pair of gangsters!" Bob was very angry.
"On the other hand," Lys said, "The whole thing has a pretty sad background. Tony's father, an Italian immigrant, lost all of his sav-

1 to blow one's lid: ausrasten, die Fassung verlieren
2 loudmouth: Großmaul
3 anger: Ärger
4 after all: letztendlich
5 exam results: Prüfungsnoten
6 lecture: Klasse, Vortrag
7 trap: *(hier)*Klappe
8 excitedly: aufgeregt
9 suspect: Verdächtiger
10 to argue: streiten
11 to accuse someone: jmd. beschuldigen

ings[1]. He made the mistake of trusting[2] gangsters who pretended to build a soccer stadium in Colorado."

The girls looked around. "The first case solved by the Three !!!" When nobody said anything Kelly smiled bashfully[3]. "Hopefully also the last one," Justus said. And he tried hard to glower[4] at them. Secretly he thought about inviting the girls to gigantic helpings of ice cream sundaes[5]. But they didn't have to know that just yet.

Satisfied they listened to Peter's report about the live match. There were only commercial breaks before the kick-off, during the break and after the final whistle. Then it was Justus' turn[6] to tell them about his visit to Mr Bow and the pursuit[7] in Santa Monica. "We have to go back there," Justus said and shrugged when he looked at Peter and his leg in a plaster cast. "Too bad you're out of commission[8]. Someone could recognize Bob and me."

Once more Lys had the solution that rescued[9] them. "I could put make-up on one of you as a disguise[10]." she suggested. The Three Investigators looked at her doubtfully[11]. "Really, I can do it!" She turned towards Bob. "It works best with your blond hair. After an hour of work not even your parents would recognize you." Justus thought Lys was adorable[12]. But he agreed to her plan not only because of that. "The best way would be if you call Sax Sendler. Ask him if, one morning, he can introduce you as his junior assistant who is work-

1 savings: Ersparnisse
2 to trust: vertrauen
3 bashful: verlegen
4 to glower: drohend schauen, finster blicken
5 helpings of ice cream sundaes: Eisbecher Portionen
6 Justus' turn: Justus war dran
7 pursuit: Verfolgung
8 out of commission: außer Gefecht
9 to rescue: retten
10 disguise: Verkleidung
11 doubtful: zweifelnd
12 adorable: hinreißend

ing on a special assignment[1] for an advertising customer," he said to Bob.

Detective question 6

Wieso ist Mr Bow plötzlich so schweigsam? Welche Spur führt die ??? trotzdem zum Ziel?

1 assignment: Auftrag

7. A Risky Bluff

Bob arrived at Eric Randolph's office without any problems. The TV journalist's secretary asked him to wait a few more minutes. Instead of sitting down in one of the visitors' chairs, he looked at his reflection in the mirrored plate glass windows[1]. A stranger with a mustache[2] looked back at him, Elizabeth did a good job. Still, he felt nervous.

The padded[3] door of the ante-room[4] opened. The gray-haired man approached him energetically; his hand was stretched out for a handshake. "Mr Sendler," Eric Randolph said with a jovial smile, "Nice to meet you."

Bob answered in the same melodic tone as Mr Randolph, who told him first of all that they unfortunately couldn't have lunch together. This was because the sprinting star Carl Lewis agreed to give a live interview on the subject of doping – only after very tough negotiations[5]. Then they chatted[6] about music agencies, a familiar topic for Bob. "Let's get to the point," he finally said. "As you know I'm acting on behalf of[7] a group of clients. They are interested in advertising in the new professional soccer league. That means in stadiums, on sportswear[8] and especially on TV." "Do you like soccer?" Mr Randolph asked.

Bob smiled at him self-confidently[9]. "I prefer baseball. But personal hobbies don't count. This is about our clients. And about business."

1 mirrored plate glass windows: verspiegelte Fensterscheiben
2 mustache: Schnurrbart
3 padded: gepolstert
4 ante-room: Vorzimmer
5 tough negotiations: zähe Verhandlungen
6 to chat: sich unterhalten, plaudern
7 on behalf of: im Interesse von
8 sportswear: Sportbekleidung
9 self-confident: selbstbewusst

If I really thought that way, Bob reflected, I'd slap[1] myself. "But I know quite a bit about soccer."

"Your agency, Sendler, represent[2] 'Sany' and 'Multisonic', if I'm not mistaken.'

Bob nodded.

"Wealthy clients[3]!" The gray-haired man slowly shook his head.

"Strong financial background," Bob agreed. He was starting to like this act. But he also had his doubts[4] if this conversation would result in anything at all, if they continued to beat about the bush[5] like that. He decided to attack head-on[6]. "We're very interested," he continued, "... although ..."

"Although?"

"We're not interested in the European concept. In any case[7] not in this country." Bob hesitated and waited for a reaction.

The man who was looking at him raised his eyebrows. "European concept? What are you talking about, young man?"

Bob didn't let the strict tone of the rebuke[8] upset him.

"I assume[9] we both know what I mean," he answered and kept a straight face. "A flop such as 'Earphone' is out of the question." He watched the head of sports, who didn't move a muscle when he heard the keyword 'earphone'. But it was even more telling[10] that he didn't react and ask about it. Instead, he went to the tall steel-cabinet[11] next to the door and took out a dark-blue folder[12].

1 to slap: ohrfeigen
2 to represent: vertreten
3 wealthy clients: zahlungskräftige Kunden
4 doubt: Zweifel
5 to beat about the bush: um den heißen Brei herumreden
6 he decided to attack head-on: er entschied sich zum Frontalangriff
7 in any case: auf jeden Fall, jedenfalls
8 rebuke: Vorwurf, Zurückweisung
9 to assume: annehmen
10 telling: *hier*: verräterisch
11 steel-cabinet: Stahlschrank
12 folder: Ordner

"We want to establish[1] commercial breaks at prearranged[2] times."
"That's out of the question. The FIFA would never agree to that."
"Then we'll just have to follow a different track[3]."
Bob slowly sat up straight. "And your TV channel knows what that means." He said this on purpose as a statement[4], not as a question. Randolph nodded. "Tell your clients that ITN TV is in control." He tapped the folder with the dossier. "We're clear for take-off[5]". For a moment he seemed to think about showing his visitor the very important documents. But then he walked back to the cabinet, put the file inside and locked it with a small key from his large bunch of keys. Then he turned around to Bob and smiled down at him in a friendly way. "From our point of view[6] a meeting can already take place next week."
Bob stood up. "I'll talk to my clients and then contact you."
The telephone rang. Randolph answered it. "Oh," he said briefly. "I'm coming." He put down the receiver. "Mr Sendler, you'll have to excuse me because Mr Lewis just arrived. I have to go to the studio." He pressed a button to switch[7] his phone to the secretary's office.
"We're finished anyway," Bob said and stretched out his hand.
"We're walking in the same direction," Randolph said and he held out his arm offering his visitor to lead the way[8]. Over his shoulder Bob looked at the cabinet with longing[9]. On their way Randolph chatted about the problems he had persuading[10] Lewis to come for an interview. Bob only half-listened. Passing by, he saw a restroom and had

1 to establish: einführen
2 prearranged: vorher vereinbart
3 track: Weg
4 statement: Aussage
5 take-off: Abflug
6 from our point of view: aus unserer Sicht
7 to switch: umschalten
8 to lead the way: vorausgehen, anführen
9 with longing: sehnsüchtig
10 to persuade: überreden

a stroke of genius[1]. Randolph was in a hurry and would hardly wait for him to return from a certain private chamber[2].

23 "Mr Randolph," he said and stopped, "I'm sorry but ... I ... erm ... need to ...," he winked at him.

"Of course." Randolph pointed to the end of the hallway. "Back there. Later you can take the elevator[3] to the first floor and you'll end up right in front of the exit." They shook hands and Bob marched down the hallway. Then he slipped[4] into the restroom and waited. After a minute he went back the same way that they came from. Many offices were empty. Some are working in the studio, Bob thought and others are at the snack-bar. Most of them want to see the world-famous Carl Lewis. Bob arrived at Randolph's ante-room, went inside and discovered a low filing-cabinet[5]. He could open five drawers easily, but not the sixth drawer labelled[6] 'correspondence'. Bob stared at the padded door leading into Randolph's office. I can't get the blue folder, he thought, but maybe something else that is interesting. He pressed down the door knob using a handkerchief – and at the same moment he heard voices. He slipped into the boss' office and left the door open a crack.

"... dinner together," a woman said. "Gladly," the other voice answered, without doubt Randolph's secretary. Bob felt sweat underneath his glued-on[7] mustache. He clenched his teeth and made a quick decision[8]. He went to the desk and switched the telephone line back on. Surely the secretary hadn't noticed yet that Randolph had switched the calls to her phone. He used the handkerchief to avoid[9]

1 stroke of genius: Geniestreich, Eingebung
2 certain private chamber: das gewisse Örtchen
3 elevator (US): Lift
4 to slip: schlüpfen
5 filing-cabinet: Aktenschrank
6 labelled: beschildert
7 glued-on: angeklebt
8 decision: Entscheidung
9 to avoid: vermeiden

fingerprints, took the receiver[1], put it down on the desk and dialled a few digits[2]. The secretary should believe that her boss was making phone calls. Then he went to the door, hesitated briefly and opened it. "Mr Randolph needs the Smell correspondence," he said with a firm voice[3].

The secretary looked up surprised. Come on, Bob was thinking, don't be surprised, just do what I tell you to do.

"All of it?"

This question wasn't a part of Bob's plan. His blood was throbbing[4] behind his temples[5]. "All of it?" he called into Randolph's empty office. Then he took a few steps backwards to be out of her range of vision[6]. He waited five seconds, then appeared again.

"Only the one with Mike Hammer," he heard himself say. He felt dizzy[7]. But he was still alert enough to bat his eyelashes[8] at the secretary to get her confidence[9].

Silently she took a key out of the pocket of her jacket, stood up and opened the sixth drawer. "Will you give it to him?"

"Will do," Bob answered, took the gray folder and disappeared into Randolph's office. He pulled out the handkerchief again, put down the receiver, but immediately took it off the hook[10] again and dialled a few numbers. He wanted the secretary to believe that her boss was busy[11] making phone calls.

"Mike Hammer,"Bob repeated in a low voice. He took a first look at the letters and whistled through his teeth. He would let Justus and

1 receiver: Telefonhörer
2 digit: Ziffer
3 with a firm voice: mit fester Stimme
4 to throb: pochen
5 temple: Schläfe
6 range of vision: Blickfeld
7 dizzy: schwindlig
8 to bat one's eyelashes: blinzeln, mit den Wimpern klimpern
9 confidence: Zutrauen
10 to take it of the hook: das Telefon abnehmen
11 busy: beschäftigt

Peter celebrate him properly for this stroke of genius and breakneck[1] manoeuvre ... If he ever got out of here again.

On the way to the taxi Justus wanted to know what happened. But Bob took bigger and bigger steps, so he couldn't keep up with him[2]. Justus hated not being in the know and he knew exactly that Bob knew that. Even in the taxi Bob didn't say a word. Instead he pressed his finger to his lips and pointed to the taxi driver who could hear every word. He also turned around a few times. He was afraid of being followed.

When they got out of the taxi Justus was almost bursting[3] with curiosity. "That's enough," he said angrily and flopped on the passenger seat of Bob's VW-beetle. "Stop the showing-off[4]. I want to know what's going on!"

Bob started to tell him the whole story and the longer he spoke, the more[5] Justus' anger disappeared. By the end he was enthusiastic. "And how did you sneak[6] past the secretary?" he finally asked.

"Slowly, slowly!" Bob wanted to enjoy[7] the situation a bit longer. "Look at this." He opened his shirt buttons and took out the folder that was slightly bent[8]. "Here you are!" he said and pressed the correspondence with Mike Hammer into his hands. "I pretended her boss had a very important phone call and that he shouldn't be disturbed[9]. So I shoved[10] the folder underneath my shirt, put my finger to my lips and tiptoed around her. I pointed to his room with my

1 breakneck: halsbrecherisch
2 to keep up with him: mit ihm Schritt halten
3 to burst: platzen
4 to show off: angeben
5 the longer ... the more: je länger ... desto mehr
6 to sneak: schleichen
7 to enjoy: genießen
8 bent: verbogen
9 to be disturbed: gestört werden
10 to shove: schieben

thumb and with an important expression on my face and said goodbye. She nodded understandingly and I was out of there."
"Ugh[1]," Justus moaned. "Not bad."
Bob's face was radiant[2].
Justus quickly looked over several letters and was very surprised. Hammer and Randolph were in cahoots with each other. The former center forward was Smell's contact to the TV channel. They unashamedly[3] offered to interrupt soccer games for commercial breaks on purpose.
"And, I bet you, he is not doing this alone," Bob said and took the exit to Rocky Beach.

24 "Your visitor is here," Peter's mother said when she opened the door. "He's waiting on the terrace." She looked at Bob closely. "Really unbelievable[4]... the way you look[5]!" And then she said that he had to remove his disguise.
"You can go inside," she said to Justus.
"And who says so?" Justus asked confused.
"My son," Mrs Shaw answered. I have no idea, what it's all about. You'll just have to trust him."
Bob left reluctantly[6] and Justus marched out to the terrace.
Peter sat there in his deck chair and pointed behind himself towards the garden.
"Cotta!" Justus called surprised. "I have to talk to you," the inspector said. "Where's Bob?" "He'll be here soon," Justus said. "We'll tell him everything. "

1 ugh: Uff *(Umgangssprache)*
2 radiant: strahlend
3 unashamed: ohne Scham, unverfroren
4 unbelievable: unglaublich
5 the way you look: wie du aussiehst
6 he left reluctantly: er ging widerstrebend

"Peter already knows about it," the inspector said. "The Smell thing is over. For you guys at least."
Justus nodded and was about to answer. At the same instant he felt a kick against his shin[1]. "What does that mean?" he asked – quickly changing his question.
"You're out[2] because someone else is involved. And we can't endanger[3] this person."
"An undercover agent[4]," Peter helped the inspector explain.
"One of the license plate numbers that you sent by fax matched the blue Ford. But not only that. It caused[5] quite a stir[6] in our police department and on our computers."
Bob came out of the house. Besides a few dark stains[7] and the glasses he looked like his old self[8] again. He also received a kick as a greeting, so he knew immediately that they had to be very careful what they said.
"We're out of the Smell case," Justus said.
"I can trust you," Cotta continued. "It's about a stock fraud[9]. A gigantic story that is going on in several states. The colleagues need two or three more days. By all means, they want to prevent[10] the responsible people from getting away with it[11]."
Justus grinned at Cotta sourly. "That is exactly what we wanted as well."

1 shin: Schienbein
2 you're out: ihr seid draußen
3 to endanger: gefährden
4 undercover agent: verdeckter Ermittler
5 to cause: verursachen
6 stir: Aufruhr
7 stain: Fleck
8 self: Selbst
9 stock fraud: Aktienschwindel
10 to prevent: verhindern
11 to get away with it: damit durchkommen

"Peter already informed me about the cheating in sports. Very interesting." He shrugged. "But I have orders from the top[1]. This story about stock is more important."
They were interrupted by the sound of the door bell. "The girls," Peter said. Cotta stood up. "So, I hope this is clear. From now on[2] you stay away from Smell, alright? I'm really sorry." He looked at them sternly[3] one more time and shook hands with each single one of them. How formal, Justus thought, the police have an agreement[4] with the Three Investigators. At the terrace door Cotta almost bumped into Lys. She held a cell phone in her hand. Elizabeth and Kelly crowded[5] in behind her. They didn't know Cotta and since[6] he walked past them so quickly Justus didn't introduce him. Justus pressed his lips together. Lys saw that and understood immediately. She waited until they heard the front door close.
"You forgot the cell phone at my place[7]," Lys said. "Jimboy called an hour ago. He wants to meet you at the junkyard this evening."

Detective question 7

Wieso gerät Bob in Schwierigkeiten – noch dazu in Verkleidung? Und mit welchem Bluff rettet er die Situation?

1 orders from the top: Befehle von oben
2 from now on: ab jetzt
3 stern: streng
4 agreement: Vereinbarung, Einigung
5 to crowd: drängeln
6 since: weil
7 my place: bei mir zu Hause

8. Chicago as a Reward[1]

Jimboy entered the junkyard through the secret door in the painting of the big fire in San Francisco. He looked pale[2] and carried a duffle bag over his shoulder. Justus remembered their first meeting at the airport. They greeted each other and Jimboy asked about Peter's leg. Then he dropped the duffle bag and sat down next to it on the grass.

"I quit," he said. It didn't sound sad at all, but rather[3] relieved. "I wanted you to be the first to hear about it."

The three boys pestered[4] him with questions. He told them about the excellent training at the boarding school, the good medical health care[5], but also about the tough drills and the many small attempts to pressure them. "After your call I finally understood." Jimboy tapped Justus' chest[6]. "I didn't want to realize that Hammer and a few of his colleagues are crooks[7]. I don't want a career under these circumstances[8]." He pulled a newspaper clipping[9] out of his pocket.

"I got it off of Hammer." It was a photograph of a dark-haired young man on the witness stand. "It's definitely our tactics coach. Only a couple of years younger." Jimboy looked up. "Did you steal that special DVD?" he suddenly asked.

Justus nodded. "Peter was the bad guy," he tried to joke and pointed at his leg in the plaster cast.

1 reward: Belohnung
2 pale: blass
3 rather: *hier* vielmehr, eher
4 to pester someone: bedrängen
5 medical health care: medizinische Versorgung
6 tapped Justus' chest: klopfte Justus auf die Brust
7 crook: Gauner
8 circumstance: Bedingung
9 newspaper clipping: Zeitungsausschnitt

"The punishment followed on his heels[1]."
Jimboy wanted to hear the whole story up until Cotta's appearance[2] a few hours ago.
"Why did you inform him?"
"We didn't inform him," the First Investigator corrected[3]. "We needed him because of the license plate number of the small blue Ford." They had forgotten to mention that before. "Sparkling-water[4]-bottle-blue," Peter said, who liked the monstrous word-snake.
"I see," Jimboy said. Then he pointed to the street, past the painting of the fire of San Francisco. "One of those cars is over there. Anyway, when I came here it was still there."
Bob was quickly on his way. The other two followed him, even Peter struggled[5] up.
With a low creaking sound[6] the wooden planks[7] of the secret door opened. "Sure enough,"Justus was surprised. The car was directly across the street. A woman sat behind the steering wheel and was leafing[8] through documents. Bob went up to the side window. He knocked and the female driver looked up. She put aside her reading[9] and got out of the car – a woman of medium-height[10] with long, brown, curly hair and a tight[11] jeans jacket.

1 The punishment followed on his heels: die Strafe folgte auf dem Fuß
2 appearance: Auftauchen
3 to correct: korrigieren
4 sparkling water: Mineralwasser
5 to struggle: kämpfen, abmühen
6 low creaking sound: leises Knarren
7 plank: Brett
8 to leaf through: durchblättern
9 reading: Lektüre
10 height: Größe
11 tight: eng

"I'm Tamara Mostowsky," she introduced herself. Justus had never heard such a hoarse voice[1] on a woman before. But he immediately took a liking[2] to her. "And you are the Three Investigators?"
Bob shook his head. "Only two-thirds. But if you join us, you'll meet the Third Investigator as well."

26 Even with an injured leg Peter was incredibly charming[3]. He limped to a chair and offered it to her. He himself sat down on the grass and groaned as he did so.

"What is it you want from us?" Bob asked.

"Your material," she answered in a tone that sounded like a bus driver asking for a ticket. That was too quick for Justus. "You're investigating[4] that stock and shares deal[5]?"

Tamara nodded. "To be exact, I was right on their tail[6]. They stopped me. The big bosses. They stopped me right before the finish line[7]. I hope, at least[8] they know why. But aren't you also pursuing Smell?"

"That's a totally different story!' Peter screamed.

"I know," the women said to calm him down. "That is exactly our chance." Then Tamara explained her plan. She knew that the boys were working on the soccer fraud. "How do you know?" Justus interrupted but she only shrugged. "I have my connections[9], you know how it works."

So they took her off the stock scandal. But she wanted the ruin of the responsible people at Smell by revealing the soccer fraud scandal.

1 hoarse voice: raue Stimme
2 to take a liking: Gefallen finden
3 incredibly charming: unglaublich charmant
4 to investigate: untersuchen
5 deal: Sache, Handel
6 on their tail: auf den Fersen
7 finish line: Ziellinie
8 at least: wenigstens
9 connection: Verbindung

"And what do we get out of it[1]?" Jimboy asked. "I mean, the Three Investigators."

"Good question," Tamara answered and smiled. "Actually nothing," she said, "besides the fact that you'll help catch a couple of quite evil villains[2]."

Justus pinched his lower lip. "We should discuss this alone for a sec[3]," he said. "If you'll excuse us..."

She silently stood up and walked away until she was out of ear-shot. She casually leaned against a pile of iron girders[4] to wait.

"I don't want to interfere[5]," Jimboy said, "but you guys must do this. This women knows the ropes[6]." They quickly agreed[7]. Bob fetched[8] the folder with Randolph's and Hammer's letters from the trailer and they added[9] the DVD as well.

"One thing is for sure," Justus said when they heard Tamara drive away. "This is the first case for us that ends like this. And if I have a choice[10], it's also the last one."

27 "Look at this!" Bob shouted and flung[11] a pile of newspapers on the desk in their trailer. "It's all about our case! All over the sports and business sections[12]."

Peter made a face. Actually he wanted to celebrate that he was finally rid of[13] the cast after four weeks, but now he wasn't in the mood for

1 what do we get out of it: was springt für uns dabei heraus
2 villain: Schurke
3 sec: *abbreviation for second*: Sekunde
4 iron girder: Eisenträger
5 to interfere: sich einmischen
6 to know the ropes: sich auskennen *(Redewendung)*
7 to agree: zustimmen, sich einigen
8 to fetch: holen
9 to add: hinzufügen
10 choice: Wahl
11 to fling: werfen
12 business section: Wirtschaftsteil
13 to be rid of: etwas los sein

celebrating anymore. Tamara did a thorough job. The newspapers wrote that after the exposure[1] of the soccer manipulations and stock fraud, all hell broke loose[2] at the Smell headquarters.
"And we're sitting here like spectators!" Justus angrily rocked back and forth[3] on the office chair. "As if we had nothing to do with the whole story."
Jimboy tried to calm down the Three Investigators. "But the most important thing is that they caught those crooks."
Bob murmured something about adorning oneself with borrowed plumes[4]. And he said they shouldn't let that happen. The First Investigator agreed with him. Then the telephone rang, Peter picked up the receiver and answered it. Then he didn't say anything else – except "Aha!" two times. "Of course … we'll be there," he finally stuttered[5]. "We wouldn't miss[6] it for anything!" He was so surprised by the phone call that he forgot to put down the receiver.
"We're flying to Chicago tomorrow."
"To Chicago?" Jimboy grinned sceptically. "Of course, great idea. The day after tomorrow Brazil is playing against Germany and the following day the USA against Switzerland."
"Exactly! And we will be there!" Peter put his fist[7] up in the air, as if he just won a sprinting race[8]. "That was Tamara!" he called. "We're invited[9] …"

1 exposure: Aufdeckung
2 all hell broke loose: war die Hölle los
3 back and forth: vor und zurück
4 to adorn oneself with borrowed plumes: sich mit fremden Federn schmücken *(Redewendung)*
5 to stutter: stottern
6 to miss something: verpassen, vermissen
7 fist: Faust
8 race: Rennen
9 invited: eingeladen

The end of his sentence was drowned out in cheering[1]. Bob and Justus performed a wild Indian war dance[2] – even the trailer began to rock. When everyone calmed down again Peter continued to speak. "There are two descendants[3] of Victor Sentir's, the company founder. They are silent partners[4]. They didn't have anything to do with the scandal and immediately supported the undercover agent when she presented the results[5] of our investigation."
"Tamara didn't forget us. She even suggested this trip as a reward," Peter said satisfied. "And the Three Investigators should definitely be there."
"Great!" Bob said.
"I'll come along, too." Jimboy announced. "I can't possibly leave you guys from the provincial Californian backwaters[6] alone in a metropolis[7] like Chicago. Chicago is my home town, after all. I know every nook and cranny[8] there. "
Justus cupped his chin in his hand[9]. "Under these circumstances we can get over the fact[10] that the whole world will never know what really happened and the way ..."
"You guys don't know everything yet," Peter interrupted[11] him. "The best is yet to come[12]." Justus frowned and told him not to keep them in suspense[13].

1 drowned out in cheering: ging im Jubel unter
2 Indian war dance: indianischer Kriegstanz
3 descendant: Nachkomme
4 silent partner: stiller Teilhaber
5 result: Ergebnis
6 backwaters: Provinz
7 metropolis: Metropole
8 every nook and cranny: jede Ecke
9 cupped his chin in his hand: stützte sein Kinn in die Hand
10 to get over the fact: die Tatsache verschmerzen, hinwegkommen
11 to interrupt: unterbrechen
12 the best is yet to come: das Beste kommt noch
13 keep in suspense: auf die Folter spannen

"Tamara says the girls are also invited!" A storm of cheering[1] broke out again.
"It's unbelievable what that woman knows about us," Justus was astonished[2]. He grabbed the phone and called Lys. "Cancel all our appointments!" He shouted into the receiver, "Who cares about Hollywood? Jimboy, the three of us and the Three !!! are flying East. Tomorrow. Okay?"

Detective question 8

Werden die ??? etwa von der verdeckten Ermittlerin reingelegt? Wieso überwiegt am Ende doch die Freude?

1 to cheer: jubeln
2 to be astonished: erstaunt sein

Englisch-deutsche Wortliste

about to – *kurz davor*
accommodate – *Unterkunft geben*
accompany – *begleiten*
accuse someone – *jmd. beschuldigen*
ace – *Ass*
achieve – *erreichen, schaffen*
act as if – *tun als ob*
actor – *Schauspieler*
actress – *Schauspielerin*
actually – *eigentlich, tatsächlich*
add – *hinzufügen*
administration building – *Verwaltungsgebäude*
admission form – *Anmeldeformular*
admit – *zugeben*
adorable – *hinreißend*
adorn oneself with borrowed plumes – *sich mit fremden Federn schmücken (Redewendung)*
advertisement – *Werbung, Anzeige*
advertising – *Werbung*
advice – *Ratschlag*
affair – *Affäre*
afford – *sich leisten*
after all – *letztendlich*
agree – *zustimmen, sich einigen*
agreement – *Vereinbarung, Einigung*
aim – *zielen*
air traffic controller – *Fluglotse*
alliteration – *Alliteration*

anger – *Ärger*
announce – *ankündigen*
annoy – *verärgern, nerven*
annoyance – *Ärger*
annoyed – *genervt, verärgert*
anyway – *jedenfalls, trotzdem*
appear – *auftauchen*
appearance – *Auftauchen, Aussehen*
application folder – *Bewerbungsmappe*
apply – *sich bewerben*
approach – *ansprechen, nähern*
appropriate – *passend*
argue – *streiten*
armband – *Armbinde*
around (to be) – *da sein, in der Nähe sein*
artificial – *künstlich*
assignment – *Auftrag*
associate – *verbinden mit*
association – *Vereinigung*
assume – *annehmen*
astonished (to be) – *erstaunt sein*
at least – *wenigstens*
at once – *sofort*
at the time – *damals*
attached – *befestigt*
attempt – *Versuch*
attend – *besuchen*
attentive – *aufmerksam*
attitude – *Einstellung*
attracted to – *angezogen von*
avoid – *vermeiden*

awesome – *super, fantastisch*
awful – *schrecklich, entsetzlich*
back and forth – *vor und zurück*
backwaters – *Provinz*
baggage claim area – *Gepäckausgabe*
baggy – *locker, weit*
balance sheet – *Bilanz*
baloney – *Unsinn (umgangsprachlich)*
ban – *Berufsverbot*
bar of soap – *Seifenstück*
barred – *vergittert*
bashful – *verlegen*
bat one's eyelashes – *blinzeln, mit den Wimpern klimpern*
beat about the bush – *um den heißen Brei herumreden (Redewendung)*
beat – *schlagen*
beg – *betteln*
behaviour – *Verhalten*
behind – *(Betonung auf der ersten Silbe) Hinterteil*
belong to – *gehören zu*
bench – *(Sitz-)Bank*
bent – *verbogen*
besides – *außerdem*
bet – *wetten*
bicycle kick – *Fallrückzieher*
blackmailed (to be) – *erpresst werden*
blank expression – *ausdruckslose Miene*
blanket – *Decke*
blockhead – *Holzkopf, Flegel*
blow one's lid – *ausrasten, die Fassung verlieren*
blush – *erröten*

boarding school – *Internat*
body – *Körper*
booth – *(Verkaufs)stand*
bossy – *herrisch*
bother – *stören*
bottom – *unteres*
branch – *Filiale, Zweigstelle*
brand – *Marke*
break – *(hier) Pause*
breakneck – *halsbrecherisch*
bribed (to be) – *bestochen sein*
brick – *Ziegelstein*
briefcase – *Aktentasche*
broadcast – *Sendung, Ausstrahlung*
buddy – *Kumpel*
bump into – *anrempeln*
burger – *Hamburger (Abkürzung)*
burst – *platzen*
business section – *Wirtschaftsteil*
busy – *beschäftigt*
call the shots – *das Sagen haben*
can't stand – *nicht ausstehen können*
canned milk – *Dosenmilch*
cannery – *Konservenfabrik*
canyon – *Schlucht*
cardboard – *Karton*
cash box – *Kasse*
cashier – *Kassierer/in*
castle – *(hier) Turm im Schachspiel*
casual – *sportlich, lässig*
caught in a tight space (to be) – *eng werden*

cause – *verursachen*
ceiling – *Decke*
celebrate – *feiern*
cell phone (US) – *Handy*
center forward – *Mittelstürmer*
century – *Jahrhundert*
CEO – *Abkürzung für chief executive officer – Geschäftsführer/in*
certain private chamber – *das gewisse Örtchen*
certificate – *Urkunde*
chain – *Kette*
change one's mind – *die Meinung ändern*
chase – *jagen*
chat – *sich unterhalten, plaudern*
cheat – *betrügen*
cheer – *jubeln*
cheerleading squad – *Cheerleader Gruppe, die während des Spiels tanzt und die Mannschaft anfeuert*
chess board – *Schachbrett*
Chevie – *abbreviation for Chevrolet (amerik. Automarke)*
choice – *Wahl*
choice location – *bevorzugte Lage*
circumstance – *Bedingung*
citizen – *Bürger/in*
clench – *ballen, anspannen*
club – *Keule*
clumsy – *ungeschickt*
coincidence – *Zufall*
college – *Hochschule*
command – *befehlen*
commercial break – *Werbepause*
compare with – *vergleichen mit*

compete – *am Wettbewerb teilnehmen, in Wettbewerb treten*
complain about – *sich beschweren über*
conclude – *schlussfolgern*
conclusion – *Schlussfolgerung*
concrete – *Beton*
confidence – *Zutrauen*
connect – *verbinden*
connection – *Verbindung*
conscience – *Gewissen*
consider – *erwägen, bedenken*
console someone – *jmd.besänftigen, trösten*
consult – *beraten lassen*
contagious – *ansteckend*
contents – *Inhalt*
contract – *Vertrag*
convert to – *zu ... übertreten*
converted trailer – *umgebauter Wohnwagen*
convertible – *Kabrio(lett), Auto mit Faltdach*
cool as a cucumber – *kalt wie ein Fisch (Redewendung)*
co-operate – *zusammenarbeiten, kooperieren*
correct – *korrigieren*
count on someone – *auf jmd. zählen*
counterattack – *Gegenangriff, Konter*
cover – *decken*
crack – *knacken*
crane – *recken, strecken*
crime case – *Kriminalfall*
crook – *Gauner*
crooked – *schief, krumm*
cross – *Flanke*
crowd – *drängeln*

crowded – *überfüllt*
cruciate ligament – *Kreuzband*
crutches – *Krücken*
curiosity – *Neugier*
curls – *Locken*
curtain – *Vorhang*
CV – *curriculum vitae, Lebenslauf*
day off – *ein freier Tag*
deadpan – *ausdruckslos*
deafening – *ohrenbetäubend*
deal – *Sache, Handel*
decent – *anständig*
decision – *Entscheidung*
deck chair – *Liegestuhl*
defender – *Verteidiger*
defense – *Verteidigung*
definitely – *ganz bestimmt*
delivery – *Lieferung*
depend on – *davon abhängen*
descendant – *Nachkomme*
desert – *Wüste*
destroyed – *zerstört*
determined – *entschlossen*
device – *Gerät*
dial – *wählen*
digit – *Ziffer*
dirty look – *böser Blick*
disagree – *nicht übereinstimmen*
disappear – *verschwinden*
disappointment – *Enttäuschung*
discovery – *Entdeckung*

disguise – *Verkleidung, Tarnung*
disgust – *Verachtung*
disturb – *stören*
dizzy – *schwindlig*
donate – *spenden*
doubt – *anzweifeln, sich nicht vorstellen können*
doubt – *Zweifel*
doubtful – *zweifelnd*
downtown – *Stadtzentrum*
dragon – *Drache*
draw straws – *Streichhölzchen ziehen, auslosen*
dress up – *sich verkleiden*
drift – *treiben*
drizzle – *nieseln*
duffle bag – *Kleidersack, Seemannsbeutel*
dumbbell – *Hantel*
duplicate key – *Ersatzschlüssel*
during – *während*
eager – *eifrig*
ear-shot – *Hörweite*
either ... or – *entweder ... oder*
elevator (US) – *Lift*
employee – *Angestellter*
encouraging – *aufmunternd*
endanger – *gefährden*
enjoy – *genießen*
enterprise – *Unternehmen*
entrance – *Eingang*
envious – *neidisch*
environmentally friendly – *umweltfreundlich*
envy – *Neid*

equipment – *Ausrüstung*
escape – *flüchten*
establish – *einführen*
even – *sogar*
every nook and cranny – *jede Ecke*
evil plan – *teuflischer Plan*
evil – *böse, hinterhältig*
exam results – *Prüfungsnoten*
exception – *Ausnahme*
excitedly – *aufgeregt*
exercise – *Bewegung, Training*
exit – *Ausgang*
expect – *erwarten*
explosive – *Sprengstoff*
exposure – *Aufdeckung*
expression – *Ausdruck*
fairly – *ziemlich*
fake – *vorgeben, markieren*
fault – *Schuld*
favorite (US), favourite (GB) – *lieblings-*
fee – *Gebühr*
fetch – *holen*
feud – *Fehde, Kleinkrieg*
field tracks – *Leichtathletikbahn*
figure out – *verstehen, enträtseln*
filing-cabinet – *Aktenschrank*
film director – *Regisseur/in*
fine – *Geldstrafe*
fingerprint – *Fingerabdruck*
finish line – *Ziellinie*
firm – *(hier) mit fester Stimme*

first aid room – *Erste Hilfe Raum*
flight of stairs – *eine Treppe*
fling – *werfen*
floor – *Stockwerk*
flowing traffic – *fließender Autoverkehr*
folder – *Ordner*
follow – *verfolgen*
football (British English) – *Fußball*
for once – *ausnahmsweise*
force – *Kraft*
former – *ehemalig, früher*
fortunately – *glücklicherweise*
forward – *Stürmer/in*
fought – *kämpften*
found – *gründen*
from now on – *ab jetzt*
frown – *Stirnrunzeln, Mundwinkel herunterziehen*
fuse – *Zünder*
gas station attendant (US) – *Tankwart*
general educational background – *Allgemeinbildung*
get a hold of someone – *jmd. erwischen*
get along – *miteinander auskommen*
get away with it – *damit durchkommen*
get enough of – *genug kriegen*
get lost! – *hau(t) ab!*
get over something – *über etwas hinwegkommen*
get to the point – *auf den Punkt kommen, ohne Umschweife*
giggle – *kichern*
glove compartment – *Handschuhfach*
glower – *drohend schauen, finster blicken*
glue – *Klebstoff*

gnash one's teeth – *Zähne knirschen*
goal post – *Torpfosten*
goalkeeper – *Torwart, Torfrau*
govern – *regieren*
grade – *(US) Schulnote*
graduation – *Schulabschluss*
greet – *grüßen*
greeting – *Begrüßung*
grin – *grinsen*
grip – *greifen*
groan – *stöhnen*
groceries – *Lebensmittel*
grocery store – *Lebensmittelladen*
guided – *geführt*
guilty – *schuldig*
guy – *Kerl, Typ*
handkerchief – *Taschentuch*
hardly – *kaum*
harmless – *harmlos*
harvest – *Ernte*
hate mail – *Drohbrief*
head of department – *Leiter der Abteilung*
headline – *Überschrift*
headquarters – *Hauptquartier*
heel – *Ferse*
height – *Größe*
heir – *Erbe*
helping – *Portion*
hesitate – *zögern*
hidden – *versteckt*
hide-away – *Versteck*

high school – *(US) entspricht dem Gymnasium*
highway – *(US) Autobahn*
hint – *Hinweis*
hire – *einstellen*
hiss – *zischen, fauchen*
hoarse voice – *raue Stimme*
hold one's breath – *Atem anhalten*
hoop – *Reifen*
hot scent – *heiße Fährte*
huge – *riesig*
hurdle – *Hürde*
ice cream sundae – *Eisbecher*
ignorant – *unwissend*
imagine – *sich vorstellen*
impressed – *beeindruckt*
impression – *Eindruck*
improve – *verbessern*
in any case – *auf jeden Fall*
in cahoots (to be) – *unter einer Decke stecken*
in charge (to be) – *das Sagen haben*
in common – *gemeinsam haben*
in favor of – *zugunsten von*
in one go – *auf ein Mal, in einem Rutsch*
in one voice – *wie aus einem Mund*
in return – *im Gegenzug*
in shape – *fit*
in vain – *umsonst*
include – *einschließen*
incomprehensible – *unverständlich*
inconspicuous – *unauffällig*
incredibly – *unglaublich*

Indian war dance – *indianischer Kriegstanz*
ingredient – *Zutat*
inherit – *erben*
injured – *verletzt*
innocent – *unschuldig*
inquire – *erkundigen, nachfragen*
insult – *Beleidigung*
interfere – *sich einmischen*
interrupt – *unterbrechen*
introduce someone – *jmd. vorstellen*
investigate – *untersuchen*
investigation – *Untersuchung*
investment – *Investition*
invited (to be) – *eingeladen sein*
iron girder – *Eisenträger*
irritated – *genervt*
jerk – *(hier) Schnösel, Trottel*
job aspiration – *Berufswunsch*
join someone – *mitgehen, dazugesellen*
joke – *witzeln*
joyless – *freudlos*
junkyard – *Schrottplatz*
just – *gerade eben, nur*
just as well – *(hier) genausogut*
juvenile delinquent – *jugendliche Straftäter*
keen on someone/something (to be) – *scharf auf jmd./etw. sein*
keep up with someone – *mit jmd. Schritt halten*
kick-off – *Anstoß*
kidney – *Niere*
kind – *Art*
knit one's brows – *die Stirn runzeln*

knothole – *Astloch*
know the ropes – *sich auskennen*
labelled – *beschildert*
lane – *Fahrspur*
latch – *Verschluss*
lawsuit – *Prozess*
lawyer – *Rechtsanwalt/Rechtsanwältin*
lead off – *wegführen*
lead the way – *vorausgehen, anführen*
lead – *führen*
leaf through – *durchblättern*
lease – *Pacht*
leaseholder – *Pächter/in*
lecture – *Klasse, Vortrag*
letter – *Buchstabe, Brief*
license plate – *Nummernschild*
lie – *lügen*
limp – *humpeln*
loading space – *Ladefläche*
location – *Platz*
longing (with longing) – *sehnsüchtig*
look fierce – *düster anfunkeln*
lose – *verlieren*
loudmouth – *Großmaul*
lousy – *mies*
loyal – *treu, anhänglich*
lucky (to be) – *Glück haben*
magnifying glass – *Lupe*
make it – *es schaffen*
male model – *männliches Fotomodell*
manage something – *etw. schaffen*

mansion – *Villa*
manufacturer – *Hersteller*
market value – *Marktwert*
mastermind – *Computerhirn, Genie*
matter-of-fact way – *sachliche Art und Weise*
mayor – *Bürgermeister/in*
medical health care – *medizinische Versorgung*
memorize – *auswendig lernen*
mentioned – *erwähnt*
mess – *(hier) Schweinerei*
message – *Nachricht*
metropolis – *Metropole*
mill – *Mühle*
mind – *jmd. etwas ausmachen*
mirrored plate glass windows – *verspiegelte Fensterscheiben*
miss out on something – *etwas verpassen*
miss – *verpassen, vermissen*
mixture ratio – *Mischungsverhältnis*
mix-up – *Verwechslung*
moan – *jammern, stöhnen*
mock – *sich mokieren, spotten*
momentary – *vorübergehende*
momentum – *Drall, Effet*
mood – *Laune, Stimmung*
muffled thud – *dumpfer Aufschlag*
mumble – *murmeln, nuscheln*
murmur – *murmeln*
mustache – *Schnurrbart*
mute – *stumm*
mutual – *gemeinsam*
myth of the Nibelungs – *Nibelungen-Sage*

narrow – *eng*
negotiations – *Verhandlungen*
neither … nor – *weder … noch*
nephew – *Neffe*
newspaper clipping – *Zeitungsausschnitt*
nod – *nicken*
nonsense – *Unsinn*
notice – *bemerken*
nowadays – *heutzutage*
obligated – *verpflichtet*
obviously – *offensichtlich*
occur – *geschehen*
offer – *anbieten*
old-fashioned – *altmodisch*
on behalf of – *im Interesse von*
on me – *auf meine Rechnung*
on one's tail – *auf den Fersen*
on purpose – *absichtlich*
on short notice – *kurzfristig*
opponent – *Gegner*
opportunity – *Gelegenheit*
opposite – *gegenüber*
orders from the top – *Befehl von oben*
ordinary – *gewöhnlich*
out of commission – *außer Gefecht*
out of ear-shot – *außer Hörweite*
outskirts – *Außenbezirk, Stadtrand*
overwhelm – *überfluten, überwältigen*
owner – *Besitzer/in*
padded – *gepolstert*
pair of pincers – *Pinzette*

pale – *blass*
participate – *teilnehmen*
patient – *geduldig*
pay off – *sich bezahlt machen*
pedestrian – *Fußgänger/in*
peer – *spähen, blicken*
pen pal – *Brieffreund/in*
penalty shoot-out – *Elfmeterschießen*
penalty – *Strafe, Strafstoß*
persuade – *überreden*
pester someone – *jdn. bedrängen*
piercing – *durchdringend, stechend*
pile up – *stapeln*
pinch – *zwicken*
pine-tree forest – *Pinienwald*
pity – *Mitleid*
plank – *Brett*
plant – *Fabrik*
plaster cast – *Gips*
poet – *Dichter/in*
point of view – *Sichtweise*
point to – *auf etw. zeigen*
polite – *höflich*
ponytail – *Pferdeschwanz*
postmark – *Poststempel*
powder – *Pulver, Puder*
practice – *Training*
prankster – *Witzbold*
prearranged – *vorher vereinbart*
preliminary round – *Vorrunde*
preserves – *Konserven*

pretend – *so tun als ob*
prevent – *verhindern*
profession – *Beruf*
profound – *tiefgründig*
promote – *für etwas werben*
proof – *Beweis*
protect – *beschützen*
proud – *stolz*
punch – *mit der Faust schlagen*
punishment – *Strafe*
pursue – *verfolgen*
pursuer – *Verfolger*
pursuit – *Verfolgung*
put pressure on – *Druck ausüben*
quit – *aufhören, aufgeben*
quite – *ziemlich*
race – *Rennen*
radiant – *strahlend*
rag – *Lappen*
range of vision – *Blickfeld*
rant – *schimpfen, meckern*
rather – *(hier) vielmehr*
relieved – *erleichtert*
reading – *Lektüre*
rear view mirror – *Rückspiegel*
reason – *Grund*
rebuke – *Vorwurf, Zurückweisung*
receiver – *Telefonhörer*
recognize – *erkennen*
recording – *Aufzeichnung*
referee – *Schiedsrichter*

refinery – *Raffinerie*
regular customer – *Stammkunde*
related to – *verwandt mit*
relationship – *Beziehung*
relative – *Vewandte/r*
release button – *Auslöser*
relieved – *erleichtert*
report card – *(US) Schulzeugnis*
report – *Gutachten*
represent – *vertreten*
rescue – *retten*
research – *Forschung*
resemble – *ähneln*
residential area – *Wohngebiet*
resist – *widerstehen*
responsible – *verantwortlich*
rest – *ausruhen*
restroom – *Toiletten*
result – *Ergebnis*
reveal – *aufdecken, verraten*
reward – *Belohnung*
rid of (to be) – *etwas los (sein)*
right away – *sofort*
rivalry – *Rivalität*
roasted almonds – *gebrannte Mandeln*
rock – *schaukeln, wippen*
Rose Bowl – *(hier)Name eines berühmten Football-Stadions*
safety lock – *Sicherheitsschloss*
satisfied – *zufrieden*
save – *ersparen, retten*
savings – *Ersparnisse*

scattered – *verstreut*
schedule – *Termin ansetzen*
school term – *Schulhalbjahr*
score a goal – *ein Tor schießen*
scout – *Späher*
screeching tires – *quietschende Reifen*
scrutinize – *mustern*
season – *Jahreszeit*
sec – *abbreviation for second – Sekunde*
secret passage – *Geheimgang*
security service – *Sicherheitsdienst*
self-confident – *selbstbewusst*
semi-finals – *Halbfinale*
send someone's regards – *Grüße ausrichten*
sense – *Sinn*
sentenced to (to be) – *verurteilt sein zu*
severe – *schwerwiegend*
shake one's head – *den Kopf schütteln*
shed – *Hütte*
shelf – *Regal*
shin – *Schienbein*
shore – *Ufer*
shove – *schieben*
show off – *angeben*
show up – *auftauchen*
shower – *Dusche*
shrug – *Achselzucken*
shudder – *sich schütteln, schaudern*
shuffling sound – *schlurfendes Geräusch*
side mirror – *Seitenspiegel*
sigh – *seufzen*

sign a contract – *einen Vertrag unterschreiben*
signal (a turn) – *blinken (um abzubiegen)*
silent partner – *stille/r Teilhaber/in*
since – *weil*
sixth sense – *übernatürlicher Sinn, sechster/siebter Sinn*
slap – *ohrfeigen*
slim down – *abnehmen*
slip – *schlüpfen*
slippery – *rutschig*
slow-motion – *Zeitlupe*
smell – *Geruch*
sneak – *schleichen*
sneakers – *Turnschuhe*
sneer – *höhnen*
so far – *bis jetzt*
soap, abbreviation for soap-opera – *Seifenoper, Serie*
soft-drink – *Erfrischungsgetränk*
solution – *Lösung*
solve – *lösen*
sparkling water – *Mineralwasser*
spectator – *Zuschauer/in*
speechless – *sprachlos*
spoil – *verderben*
sportswear – *Sportbekleidung*
spotlight – *Scheinwerfer*
spur on – *antreiben*
squat – *hocken*
squeal – *verpfeifen*
stack – *Stapel*
staff – *Belegschaft*
stain – *Fleck*

stamina – *Kondition*
stare – *anstarren*
statement – *Aussage*
States – *Abkürzung für United States of America*
stationery paper – *Briefpapier*
steel-cabinet – *Stahlschrank*
steering wheel – *Lenkrad*
stern – *streng*
stir – *Aufruhr*
stock fraud – *Aktienschwindel*
strand of hair – *Haarsträhne*
strange – *seltsam*
stranger – *Fremde/r*
stress something – *etw. betonen*
stretcher – *Tragbahre*
stride – *großer Schritt*
stroke of genius – *Geniestreich, Eingebung*
struggle – *kämpfen, abmühen*
stuff – *stopfen, Zeug*
stumble – *stolpern*
stutter – *stottern*
substitute – *Ersatz*
successful – *erfolgreich*
sugar-beet – *Zuckerrübe*
suggest – *vorschlagen*
suitable – *passend*
sunshade – *Sonnenschirm*
surprise attack – *Überraschungsangriff*
surrounding – *umliegend*
survive – *überleben*
suspect someone – *jmd. verdächtigen*

suspect – *Verdächtiger*
suspense – *Spannung*
swallow – *schlucken*
swear – *beschimpfen*
sweating – *schwitzend*
sweeper – *Libero*
switch – *umschalten*
tackle (a task) – *(eine Aufgabe) angehen*
take a liking – *Gefallen finden*
take-off – *Abflug*
talkative – *gesprächig*
tap – *klopfen*
technical term – *Fachausdruck*
telling – *(hier) verräterisch*
temple – *Schläfe*
testify at court – *bei Gericht aussagen*
though – *jedoch*
thread – *Faden*
throb – *pochen*
throw-in – *Einwurf*
thump – *klopfen, daraufschlagen*
tight – *eng*
time off – *Freizeit*
tiptoe – *auf Zehenspitzen gehen*
tool – *Werkzeug*
topic – *Thema*
torn – *gerissen*
tough – *zäh*
tournament – *Turnier*
tower – *Kontrollturm*
trace something back – *zurückverfolgen*

trace – *Spur*
track and field – *Leichtathletik*
track – *Pfad, Weg*
track-suit – *Trainingsanzug*
trade association – *Unternehmerverband*
traffic jam – *Verkehrsstau*
training unit – *Trainingseinheit*
transparent folder – *Klarsichthülle*
trap door – *Falltür*
treasure – *Schatz*
treat – *behandeln*
trust – *vertrauen*
try-out – *Testspiel*
tube – *Röhrchen*
turn to – *lenken auf*
unashamed – *ohne Scham, unverfroren*
unbeatable – *unschlagbar*
unbelievable – *unglaublich*
undamaged – *unbeschädigt*
undercover agent – *verdeckter Ermittler*
unfortunately – *leider*
unintelligible – *unverständlich*
unlike – *im Gegensatz zu*
upcoming – *aufstrebend*
upset – *aufgebracht*
urge – *drängen*
use – *verwenden*
used to – *früher*
van – *Lieferwagen*
varsity league – *oberste Liga einer Schule, Liga einer Universität*
verdict – *Urteil*

versatile – *vielseitig*
victim – *Opfer*
view – *Aussicht*
villain – *Schurke*
visitor – *Besucher/in*
volunteer – *etwas freiwillig tun*
wanna – *steht für 'want to'(Umgangssprache) – möchtest du*
warehouse – *Lagerhalle*
wave – *Welle*
wealthy – *wohlhabend*
whisper – *flüstern*
whistle – *Pfiff, Trillerpfeife*
wicker beach chair – *Strandkorb*
wink – *zwinkern*
witness stand – *Zeugenstand*
witness – *Zeuge/Zeugin*
work – *funktionieren, arbeiten*
worried – *besorgt*
worry – *sich Sorgen machen*
worst – *schlimmste*
would have been – *wäre gewesen*
wrinkle one's nose – *die Nase rümpfen*
wrongdoing – *Vergehen*
x-ray – *röntgen*
yawn – *gähnen*
youth work – *Sozialarbeit mit Jugendlichen*

Nützliche Detektiv-Ausdrücke

Hier sind einige Vokabeln und Redewendungen, die hilfreich sind, wenn man über Verbrechen und Detektivarbeit spricht.

arrest someone – *jemanden festnehmen*
be sent to prison – *ins Gefängnis gesteckt werden*
break into a house – *in ein Haus einbrechen*
case – *Fall*
collect evidence – *Beweismaterial/Hinweise sammeln*
commit a crime – *ein Verbrechen begehen*
commit sabotage – *Sabotage begehen*
criminal – *Krimineller, Verbrecher*
detective – *Detektiv*
discover a clue – *einen Hinweis entdecken*
drop one's weapon – *seine Waffe fallen lassen*
evidence – *Beweismaterial*
Freeze! – *Keine Bewegung!*
guilty – *schuldig*
innocent – *unschuldig*
investigate a case – *in einem Fall ermitteln*
investigation – *Ermittlung*
investigator – *ein Ermittler, eine Ermittlerin*
launch an investigation – *eine Ermittlung starten*
look out for something – *auf etwas achten*
point a gun/pistol at someone – *ein Gewehr/eine Pistole auf jemanden richten*
prove that someone is guilty/innocent – *beweisen, dass jemand schuldig/unschuldig ist*
robbery – *ein Raubüberfall, ein Diebstahl*

solve a case – *einen Fall lösen*
steal something – *etwas stehlen*
suspect – *ein Verdächtiger, eine Verdächtige*
suspicious behaviour – *verdächtiges Verhalten*
suspicious person – *eine verdächtige Person*
thief – *Dieb*
tie someone up – *jemanden fesseln*
undercover agent – *verdeckter Ermittler*
weapon – *Waffe*

Aufgaben

1 A Favorite Game

Hier werden englische Wörter umschrieben. Welche Wörter sind gemeint? Du hast eine Auswahl unten im Fußballtor. Wenn du das richtige Wort gefunden hast, trage es in die Lücke nach der Definition ein.

1. You can carry someone who is injured on it. ________________
2. It's a chance to do something. ________________
3. A girl who dances and cheers ________________
4. A player returns an attack ________________
5. A girl's name ________________
6. A person who knows the game rules perfectly and who has a whistle. ________________

· sweeper · Elton · football · opportunity · corner · referee · sandwich · cheerleader ·

chicken · player · counterattack · majesty ·

employee · stretcher · Elizabeth · junkyard

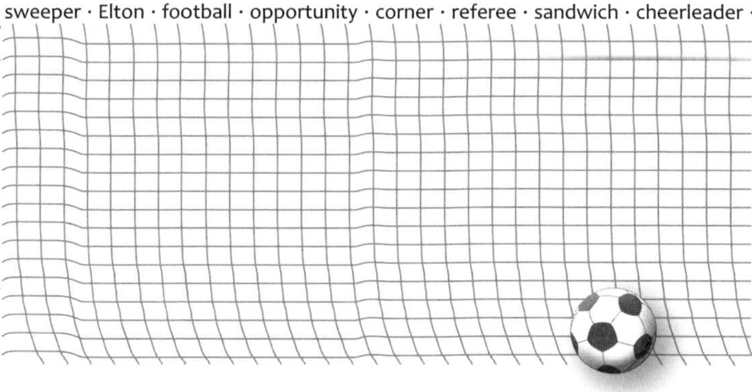

Die Anfangsbuchstaben der Wörter von 1.–6. ergeben dein Lösungswort! Trage es in die Lücke ein. ________________________

2 Nice or Not

Was meinst du: wer ist eine nette Person? Kreuze an.

	☺= nett	☹= nicht nett
1. friend		
2. jerk		
3. team mate		
4. crook		
5. show-off		
6. a gentleman		
7. idiot		
8. aunt		
9. villain		

3 Word Snake

In dieser Wortschlange sind sieben Wörter zu finden, die du beim Fußballspielen benötigst. Kreise sie ein und schreibe sie mit ihrer deutschen Übersetzung daneben.

1. ______________________________

2. ______________________________

3. ______________________________

4. ______________________________

5. ______________________________

6. ______________________________

7. ______________________________

4 Wie die Zeit vergeht!

Tipp!
Gib acht auf Signalwörter, wie z.B. gestern, heute, letzte Woche!

Adlerauge aufgepasst!
Was findet in der Gegenwart, was in der Vergangenheit statt?
Unterstreiche die richtigen Verb-Formen

1. His team mate is/was a talented soccer player now.
2. The soccer team plays/played in the varsity league last year.
3. The soccer tournament is taking/took place in Pasadena at the moment.
4. The investigator thinks/thought about the conclusion yesterday.

5 Gegenteile – Antonyms

Opposites attract – das bedeutet: „Gegenteile ziehen sich an“:
„Jimboy ist groß (*tall*) – im Vergleich zu ihm ist Justus klein (*short*).“

Detektive mit Spürsinn sind gefragt: Findest du noch weitere Gegenteile?
Verbinde die Adjektive, die das Gegenteil bedeuten.

Tipp!
Wusstest du schon, dass man Begriffe, die das Gegenteil bedeuten, auch ‚antonyms' nennt?

glad	**short**
sleepy	calm
nervous	annoyed
tall	attentive
injured	healthy

6 Word Snake

Augen auf! Finde und unterstreiche die fünf Adjektive, die in der Wortschlange versteckt sind. Wie heißen diese Worte auf deutsch?

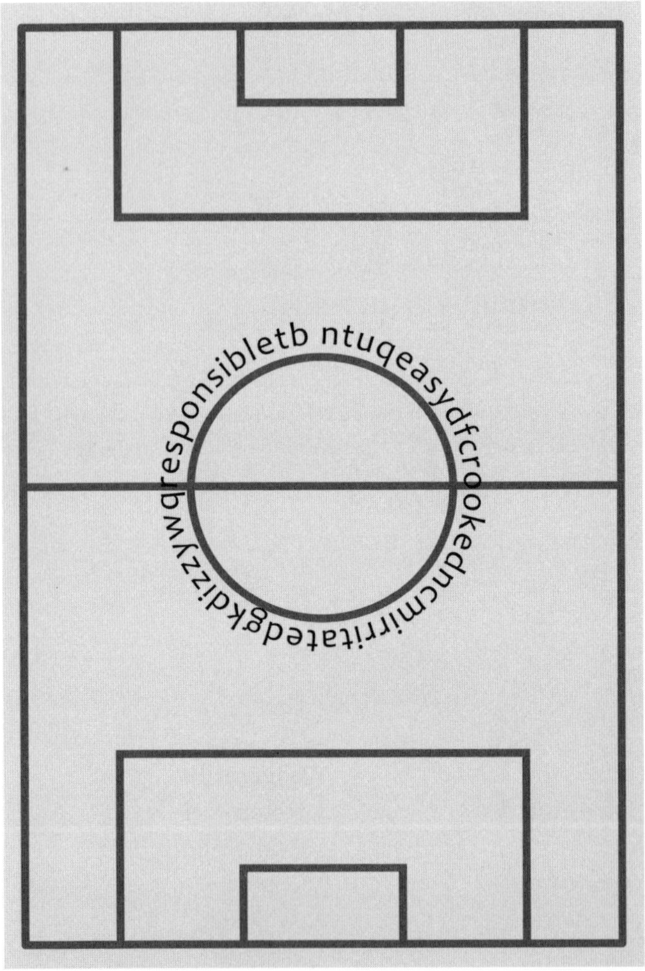

7 Crossword puzzle

Trage die englischen Begriffe ein.

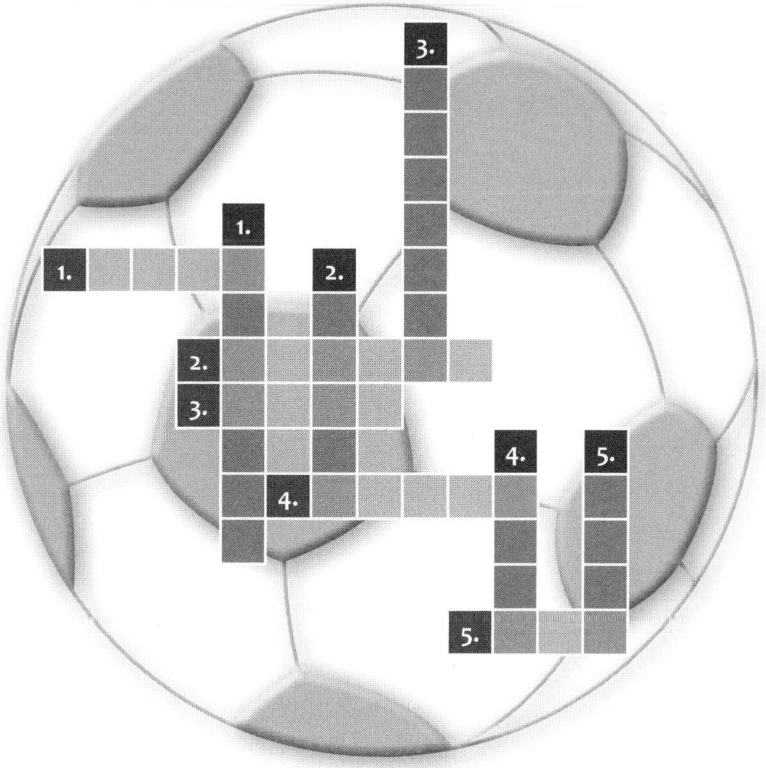

Senkrecht:
1. Anpfiff, Antritt
2. Flanke
3. Schiedsrichter
4. Mannschaft
5. Rasen, Gras

Waagerecht:
1. treten
2. Eckball, Ecke
3. wissen
4. schießen
5. Männer

8 American or British?

Tipp!
Die Sprache nähert sich in den USA und in Großbrittanien immer mehr an – manche Unterschiede verschwinden sogar mit der Zeit.

a.)
Weißt du, welche Unterschiede es zwischen amerikanischem und britischem Englisch gibt?
Verbinde die Wortpaare, welche die gleiche Bedeutung haben!

American English (AE)	*British English (BE)*

trailer	European football
truck	**mobile phone**
highway	lorry
soccer	mobile home
cell phone	motorway

b.)
Kannst du die Wörter zuordnen? Mache dich auf Spurensuche und schreibe die Abkürzung AE oder BE hinter das jeweilige Wort. (Erlaubte Detektiv-Hilfsmittel sind Wörterbuch und Internet.)

to memorize _AE_	memorise ____
theatre ____	theater ____
center ____	centre ____
in favor of ____	in favour of ____
defence ____	defense ____

9 Verwandte Wörter

Nutze deinen detektivischen Spürsinn! Schau dir die englischen Wörter genau an. Findest du die Verwandtschaft zur deutschen Sprache? Kannst du die deutsche Bedeutung erraten? Dann schreibe die deutsche Übersetzung in die Lücken.

Vorsicht – wir haben eine kleine Falle eingebaut! Eines der Wörter ist ein „falscher Freund“ (false friend) und bedeutet etwas ganz anderes als das deutsche Wort, welches ähnlich geschrieben wird. Finde den “false friend” und unterstreiche ihn.

Tipp!
Manchmal kann man die Bedeutung von Wörtern herleiten, wenn sie im Deutschen ähnlich sind. Aber Vorsicht vor ‚false friends'!

1. powder = ________________

   Er streute ______________ auf den Briefumschlag.

2. pair of pincers = ________________

   Er nahm eine __________, um den Drohbrief anzufassen.

3. rivalry = ________________

   Zwischen Fußball und Football-spielern gab es ______________.

4. patient = ________________

   Er wartete lange auf seine Chance, aber er war sehr _________.

5. to manufacture = ________________

   Die Lebensmittelfabrik sollte auch Speiseöl ________________.

6. popular = ________________

   Pele war ein ________________ Fußballer.

7. to stutter = ________________

   “Natürlich ... w-w-wir kommen,”________________ er.

Eile mit Weile.

Rom wurde auch nicht an einem Tag erbaut.

10 Sprichwörter

Oje, hier hat jemand das Detektivbüro durchsucht und ein großes Durcheinander angerichtet.
Folge deiner Spürnase! Kannst du die entsprechenden deutschen Sprichwörter wieder in die richtige Reihenfolge bringen und in die Lücken eintragen?

Money doesn't grow on trees. *Von nichts kommt nichts.*

To beat about the bush. *Um den heißen Brei herumreden.*

A rolling stone gathers no moss.

____

Practice makes perfect.

____

Not all that glitters is gold.

____

Wer rastet, der rostet.

Rome wasn't built in a day.

____

Haste makes waste.

____

Übung macht den Meister.

Es ist nicht alles Gold, was glänzt.

11 All Alliterations

Welche Sätze enthalten Alliterationen und welche Sätze Redewendungen? (Falls du nicht mehr weißt, was das ist, siehe Seite 19 und 20). Unterstreiche die Alliterationen. Dann schreibe jeweils den ersten Buchstaben der Alliterationen auf die Schreibzeile. In der richtigen Reihenfolge ergeben die Buchstaben einen Begriff aus dem Fußballstadion; trage das Lösungswort unten ein.

1. Let sleeping dogs lie. ______
2. All alliterations are allowed. ______
3. No news not nasty news. ______
4. All's well that ends well. ______
5. Five fans finish Friday. ______
6. Susan sold seven soccer socks. ______
7. Better late than never. ______

They love sports: ____________________

12 Rate, rate, was ist das!

Tipp!
Manche Wörter haben mehrere Bedeutungen!

Welche Bedeutung passt hier hinein?
Kannst du es aus dem Zusammenhang erraten?
Wähle die 1. oder 2. Bedeutung aus. Ergänze den englischen Satz und übersetze dann den Satz ins Deutsche.

a) steps or steps? *1. Schritte* *2. Stufen, Treppe*

He jumped down the stone __________.

Er ______________________________.

The tall boy took big __________.

Der großgewachsene ____________________.

b) mean or mean? *1. bedeuten 2.böse, gemein*

The referee was a ____________ man.

Der Schiedsrichter ______________________________________.

Soccer ____________s 'Fußball' in German.

Fußball ______________________________________.

c) miss or miss? *1. verpassen, verfehlen 2. vermissen*

The soccer player ____________ ed a cross.

Der ______________________________________.

The traveller ____________ ed his old friends.

Der Reisende ______________________________________.

d) jerk or jerk *1. Trottel, Schnösel 2. Ruck*

'What a ____________!' the First Investigator said.

'Was für ein ____________!' sagte ____________________.

With one ____________ he pulled the string off the fuse.

Mit einem ______________________________ von dem Auslöser.

Lösungen

Die Antworten zu den Detektiv-Fragen findest du selbst heraus. Hier gibt es keine Bewertung, kein richtig oder falsch. Deine eigene Meinung ist hier gefragt!

1. A Favorite Game

1. You can carry someone who is injured on it. **stretcher**
2. It's a chance to do something. **opportunity**
3. A girl who dances and cheers. **cheerleader**
4. A player returns an attack **counterattack**
5. A girl's name **Elizabeth**
6. A person who knows the game rules perfectly and who has a whistle. **referee**

~~chicken, player,~~ counterattack, ~~majesty, sweeper, Elton, football~~, opportunity, ~~corner,~~ referee, ~~sandwich,~~ cheerleader, ~~employee~~, stretcher, Elizabeth, ~~junkyard~~

Lösungswort: soccer

2. Nice or Not

1. friend ☺ = Freund/in
2. jerk ☹ = Trottel, Schnösel
3. team mate ☺☹ > Ein/e Mitspieler/in kann beides sein – nice or not nice.
4. crook ☹ = Gauner, Betrüger
5. show-off ☹ = Angeber/in
6. gentleman ☺ = Kavalier, Ehrenmann
7. idiot ☹ = Schwachkopf, Idiot
8. aunt ☺☹ > Das ist Glücksache – eine Tante kann beides sein – nice or not nice.
9. villain ☹ = Bösewicht, Gauner

3. Word Snake

Xw **1.** cross lr **2.** sweeper mn **3.** forward ztp **4.** penalty kl **5.** kick ecy **6.** goal bv **7.** defense bnh

1. Flanke, 2. Libero, 3. Stürmer, 4. Strafe, Strafstoß, 5. Schuss, schießen, kicken, 6. Tor, 7. Verteidigung

4. Wie die Zeit vergeht!

1. His team mate is/~~was~~ a talented soccer player now.
2. The soccer team ~~plays~~/played in the varsity league last year.
3. The soccer tournament is taking/~~took~~ place in Pasadena at the moment.
4. The investigator ~~thinks~~/thought about the conclusion yesterday.

5. Gegenteile – Antonyms

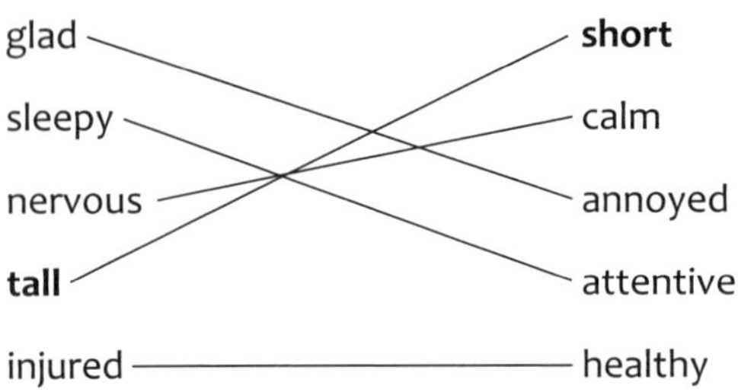

6. Word Snake

Ntuq **1.** easy df **2.** crooked ncm **3.** irritated gk **4.** dizzy wq **5.** responsible tb

1. leicht, 2. krumm, 3. genervt, 4. schwindlig, 5. verantwortlich

7. Crossword puzzle

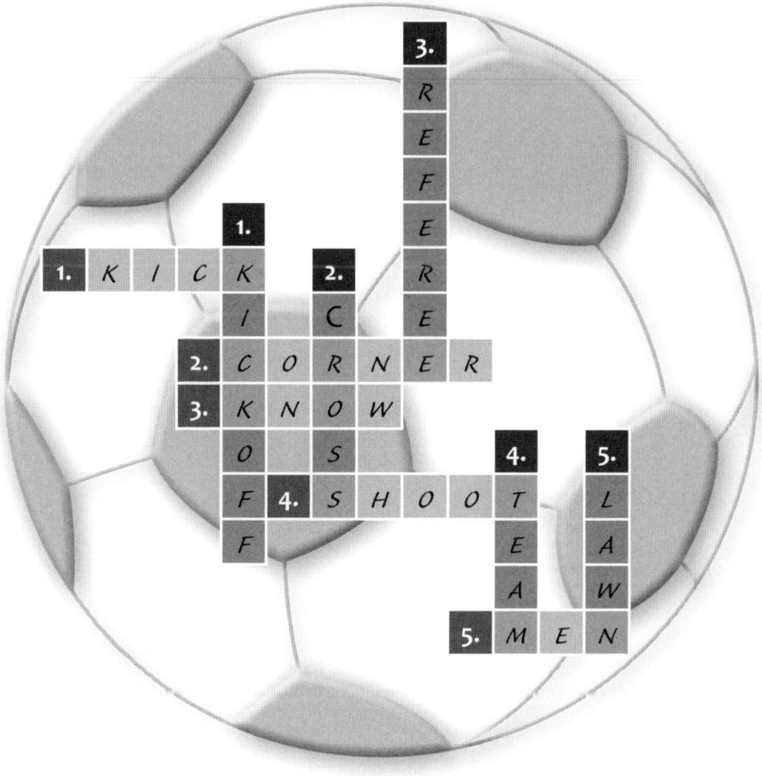

Senkrecht:

1. Anpfiff, Antritt	*kick-off*
2. Flanke	*cross*
3. Schiedsrichter	*referee*
4. Mannschaft	*team*
5. Rasen, Gras	*lawn*

Waagerecht:

1. treten	*kick*
2. Eckball, Ecke	*corner*
3. wissen	*know*
4. schießen	*shoot*
5. Männer	*men*

8. American or British?

a.)

American English	*British English*
Wohnwagen = trailer	European football
LKW = truck	**mobile phone**
Autobahn = highway	lorry
Fußball = soccer	mobile home
Handy = cell phone	motorway

b.)

auswendig lernen	= to memorize	**AE**	memorise	**BE**
Theater	= theatre	**BE**	theater	**AE**
Zentrum, Mittelpunkt	= center	**AE**	centre	**BE**
zugunsten von	= in favor of	**AE**	in favour of	**BE**
Verteidigung	= defence	**BE**	defense	**AE**

9. Verwandte Wörter

1. powder = *Pulver, Puder*
   Er streute *Pulver* auf den Briefumschlag.
2. pair of pincers = *Pinzette*
   Er nahm eine *Pinzette*, um den Drohbrief anzufassen.
3. rivalry = *Rivalität*
   Zwischen Fußball- und Football-spielern gab es *Rivalität*.

4. patient= *geduldig*
   Das ist der „falsche Freund“ – es kann nämlich geduldig oder Patient bedeuten!
   Er wartete lange auf seine Chance, aber er war sehr *geduldig*.

5. manufacture = *herstellen*
   Die Lebensmittelfabrik sollte auch Speiseöl *herstellen*.

6. popular = *populär, beliebt*
   Pele war ein *beliebter* Fußballer.

9. to stutter = *stottern*
   "Natürlich ... w-w-wir kommen," *stotterte* er.

10. Sprichwörter

Money doesn't grow on trees.	*Von nichts kommt nichts.*
A rolling stone gathers no moss.	*Wer rastet, der rostet.*
Practice makes perfect.	*Übung macht den Meister.*
Not all that glitters is gold.	*Es ist nicht alles Gold, was glänzt.*
Rome wasn't built in a day.	*Rom wurde auch nicht an einem Tag erbaut.*
Haste makes waste.	*Eile mit Weile.*
to beat about the bush	*um den heißen Brei herumreden*

11. All Alliterations

1. Let sleeping dogs lie. (*Schlafende Hunde soll man nicht wecken.*)
2. All alliterations are allowed.> Der zweite Buchstabe ist A.
3. No news not nasty news.> Der dritte Buchstabe ist N.
4. All's well that ends well. (*Ende gut, alles gut.*)
5. Five fans finish Friday.> Der erste Buchstabe ist F.
6. Susan sold seven soccer socks. > Der vierte Buchstabe ist S.
7. Better late than never. (*Besser spät, als nie.*)

They love sports: **FANS**

12. Rate, rate, was ist das!

a) steps or steps? *1. Schritte 2. Stufen, Treppe*
He jumped down the stone steps.
*Er sprang die **Steinstufen** hinunter.*
The tall boy took big steps.
*Der großgewachsene Junge nahm große **Schritte**.*

b) mean or mean? *1. bedeuten 2. böse, gemein*
The referee was a mean man.
*Der Schiedsrichter war ein **gemeiner** Mann.*
Soccer means 'Fußball' in German.
*Fußball **bedeutet** Fußball auf deutsch.*

c) miss or miss? *1. verpassen, verfehlen 2. vermissen*
The soccer player missed a cross.
*Der Fußballspieler hat eine Flanke **verfehlt**.*
The traveller missed his old friends.
*Der Reisende **vermisste** seine Freunde.*

d) *jerk* or *jerk* — *1. Trottel, Schnösel* *2. Ruck*

'What a jerk!' the First Investigator said.

'Was für ein **Trottel!'** *sagte der Erste Detektiv.*

With one jerk he pulled the string off the fuse.

Mit einem **Ruck** *zog er die Schnur von dem Auslöser.*

Die drei ???® ... ihre großen Fälle!

- ☐ Angriff der Computerviren
978-3-440-11674-6
- ☐ Fußball-Gangster
978-3-440-11675-3
- ☐ Vampir im Internet
978-3-440-11676-0
- ☐ Insektenstachel
978-3-440-11677-7
- ☐ Tal des Schreckens
978-3-440-11678-4
- ☐ Hexenhandy
978-3-440-11679-1
- ☐ Gift per E-Mail
978-3-440-11680-7
- ☐ und der Schatz der Mönche
978-3-440-11681-4
- ☐ Die sieben Tore
978-3-440-11682-1
- ☐ Das Auge des Drachen
978-3-440-11683-8
- ☐ Villa der Toten
978-3-440-11684-5

- ☐ Der namenlose Gegner
978-3-440-11877-1

- ☐ Auf tödlichem Kurs
978-3-440-11685-2
- ☐ Der finstere Rivale
978-3-440-11686-9
- ☐ Das düstere Vermächtnis
978-3-440-11687-6
- ☐ Der schwarze Skorpion
978-3-440-11688-3
- ☐ und der Geisterzug
978-3-440-11692-0
- ☐ Spur ins Nichts
978-3-440-11693-7
- ☐ Fußballfieber
978-3-440-11691-3
- ☐ Schrecken aus dem Moor
978-3-440-11689-0
- ☐ Geister-Canyon
978-3-440-11690-6
- ☐ SMS aus dem Grab
978-3-440-11695-1
- ☐ Schatten über Hollywood
978-3-440-11696-8
- ☐ Schwarze Madonna
978-3-440-11694-4
- ☐ Fluch des Drachen
978-3-440-11698-2
- ☐ Spuk im Netz
978-3-440-11697-5
- ☐ Haus des Schreckens
978-3-440-11699-9
- ☐ Fluch des Piraten
978-3-440-11701-9
- ☐ Fels der Dämonen
978-3-440-11700-2

- ☐ Der tote Mönch
978-3-440-11703-3
- ☐ und das versunkene Dorf
978-3-440-11705-7
- ☐ Pfad der Angst
978-3-440-11702-6
- ☐ Die geheime Treppe
978-3-440-11704-0
- ☐ Das Geheimnis der Diva
978-3-440-11708-8
- ☐ und die Fußball-Falle
978-3-440-11706-4
- ☐ Stadt der Vampire
978-3-440-11707-1
- ☐ Zwillinge der Finsternis
978-3-440-11548-0
- ☐ und die Poker-Hölle
978-3-440-11567-1
- ☐ Tödliches Eis
978-3-440-11568-8
- ☐ Grusel auf Campbell Castle
978-3-440-11920-4
- ☐ Die Rache der Samurai
978-3-440-11906-8
- ☐ Der Biss der Bestie
978-3-440-11919-8
- ☐ Das Gespensterschloss
978-3-440-11921-3
- ☐ Schwarze Sonne
978-3-440-11875-7
- ☐ und die feurige Flut
978-3-440-11876-4

Jeder Band mit 128 Seiten
Je €/D 7,95
Preisänderung vorbehalten

www.kosmos.de/die_drei_fragezeichen

KOSMOS